D1310604

A
SWAN
VALLEY
Journal

by
Edward L. Foss

SkyHouse Publishers

Library of Congress Catalog Card Number 94-71889

ISBN 1-56044-306-5

Published by Edward L. Foss, Condon, Montana,
in cooperation with SkyHouse Publishers,
an imprint of Falcon Press, Helena, Montana.

Distributed by Falcon Press,
P. O. Box 1718, Helena, Montana 59624,
phone 1-800-582-2665.

First Edition
Manufactured in the United States of America

CONTENTS

ACKNOWLEDGMENTS

I should like to thank friends to whom I feel deeply indebted —

Noelle Sullivan, editor, whose kindness, understanding, tact and encouragement meant very much to me.

Gloria Busch, who drew the original sketch of the "home place" from which the drawing at each chapter head was taken.

Suzanne Vernon, who typed the original manuscript, offered encouragement and made many useful suggestions.

Claudia Kux, for her part in leading me to editor and publisher.

Cal Tassinare, wilderness ranger, who by word and example instructed me in the proper use of fragile highcountry wilderness and in mountain travel.

Special thanks to friends who offered encouragement and urged me to publish. You know who you are!

MY MOUNTAIN WORLD

I watched as the pickup truck rounded a bend in the road and was gone. Sounds from its motor were deadened by the wet, heavy snow that drove the carpenters home while they thought they still had some chance of getting there. The autumn storm had begun suddenly and had toppled a tree over a power line somewhere in the forest, leaving me without electricity. I brushed snow from my head and shoulders, its heavy, wet flakes adding their weight to the gracefully bending, snow-loaded branches of a fir tree near me. Enjoying the longed-for feeling of isolation in the storm's aftermath, I couldn't ignore a growing feeling of concern—my cabin and barn were both unfinished, I had no heat, and the horses had no hay. Not a fence on the place would hold stock. It was September 15, 1965. Would I be able to settle into the Swan Valley before winter arrived to stay?

I was, and many good days have passed since that wintry September one. I remember another: a June day that was bright and warm. I had finished my work in the cabin, had stripped off my sweat suit, and was ready to dress when a glance outside showed me that both horses had eaten their fill in the lower meadow and were standing at the fence, waiting for pellets. On impulse I slipped galoshes over my bare feet, picked up the binoculars, and walked to the barn in the nude. As I wandered slowly back toward the cabin, enjoying the feel of air and sunlight on my body, I suddenly began to chuckle. I pictured the surprise of any visitor who might have found me wandering about in the buff, galoshes on my feet and binoculars hanging from a strap around my neck. Does age, I wondered, give one license to be so unconventional?

For more than twenty-seven years I've conducted a shameless love affair with this Swan Valley setting, the two mountain ranges and mountain valley I call my home. I am not the first one to choose this place. Old Joe Buerger homesteaded on the same land in 1918-1919, clearing the specified number of acres, building himself a cabin of logs, and filing claim. Joe was unmarried. He planted fruit trees and a garden, and is said to have been a lover of flowers. "Young fry" of his day seem to have been most impressed by Joe's phonograph and stack of records. My abstract tells me that he died on or about April 25, 1928. Valley folk built a pine box and buried him on the place he had worked. Since Joe left no heirs, his personal possessions and his land (appraised at $1,200) reverted to the county. Six months later county authorities asked for a reappraisal since no one would buy the property at that high figure. The property was reappraised; its new value $750. It sold.

After Joe's time the property had several owners, none of whom appeared to have given it any care. When I saw the place for the first time, nearly forty years after Joe's death, his original sod-roofed homesteader's cabin lay collapsed and partially covered with hop vines. Other log buildings on the grounds were in a state of disrepair; the meadow was over-grazed, and rubbish lay everywhere. The litter of logging, together with five huge piles of partially burned sawdust and slabs, completed the picture of destruction. But when I lifted my eyes from the litter at my feet, I saw a very blue Montana sky gently caressing the peaks of two mountain ranges. Looking around, I found many water-filled potholes on the property, as well as scattered areas of untouched forest, and decided there should be little reason for me to be idle or bored in this place.

In many ways living in these woods is like returning to college, since there is knowledge here to be gained by the naturally curious. Although much can be learned while sitting at a cabin window, many more things can be discovered only in the field. Here, as in college, the quality of learning depends upon the effort expended and the mind's wide-open door. In these mountains the fortunate few who retain their childhood sense of wonder find excitement.

There is also pleasure to be found in these hills, with each season. In spring, deer return to the blocks, wildflowers bloom, and water roars in the creeks. I find great excitement in the thawing of each pond, since this means the return of courting, fighting, nesting ducks. I notice all birds as they return to the area, but somehow the flash of blue marking the first bluebird of the season causes me greater joy than most of the others. Just knowing that bluebirds are here and that they may nest in the meadow does much toward making spring a success.

Other creatures contribute to the seasonal show. Deer drop their fawns and elk calve. Ducks appear on the ponds, their tiny ducklings swimming in close formation behind them. Hummingbirds, those feisty bits of color, add their zest for life, too. On days of peak feeding, these tiny birds have taken fifteen cups of syrup from my feeders. As June begins, the playing, fighting, displaying hummingbirds are still active about the feeders. Later in the month, their work completed, the polygamous males leave the area. Folklore treasured by a few of the locals has it that these tiny birds travel south tucked away among the feathers of a goose. A charming story, but one that authorities reject. During nesting, I see hummers taking insects on the wing, but few fly to my feeders. Only later, with young in tow, the females return to the syrup for a time. We also play host to these birds in migration.

About mid-June Swainson's thrushes also make their appearance in the valley. At first only a few of their voices are heard, but by late June their chorus is complete. For perhaps an hour in early morning and again in the evening, these birds pipe songs that are of such import in both territorial relationships and courtship. Their beautiful, soul-satisfying singing is also of great importance to me.

With the arrival of summer in the valley, spring comes to

the high country. There snowmelt cascades down mountainsides, creeks roar, and multicolored flowers carpet alpine meadows. Summer down below is the season of tourists. Human visitors come north in the warm and sometimes too dry months. July and August can be fun when moisture is adequate, but in years of drought they can be frightening. I remember well the summer of 1967, reported by the Forest Service to be the worst fire season since 1910, the most dangerous fire year in its experience. Another such year, 1979, brought soaring summer temperatures day after day. Early in July of that year the nightly passage of dry electrical storms over the mountains caused some ten fires daily in the Flathead National Forest.

Winters in the Swan country are a mixed bag. Although in general we have too little sunshine, when bright days do appear they can be unbelievably beautiful. Nights of moonlight following a fresh snowfall are indescribably lovely. Here we have unlimited opportunities for snowshoeing or cross-country skiing. We also have snow to shovel, roads to plow, and ice to combat. When outside drains freeze and toilets, baths, and sinks become conversation pieces for the duration, we quickly decide whether or not we are really meant for this type of living. But even if winter becomes long, we know that with the appearance of spring the problems of winter will be mostly forgotten.

No season is completely free of worries. Even in these lovely mountains one may become dissatisfied. In spring, I start looking toward the high places and wondering if my aging legs will carry me there for another season. Beautiful Indian summer days in the fall are frequently less than perfect because of smoke from burning slash. Game, so plentiful here a few years ago, is seen less frequently now. The pressures of hunting, logging (with habitat change), and highway traffic have all played their part in decimating the deer and elk herds. The "slob" hunter is a creature on which there is no open season, neither do we have recourse against the trapper who caters to the vanity of human animals. Timber industry greed and the lack of resistance to it by the official guardians of our forests can be maddening to those of us who regard overcutting as a sin. And finally, since developers have found us, with each year more people appear in my valley paradise. Many promptly set about destroying what they have come to enjoy. At those rare moments when dissatisfaction runs high, I try to think of places I'd rather be. But I can't think of any. I've traveled no farther than 180 miles from the valley since my arrival here twenty-seven years ago.

To thoroughly enjoy life in these mountain surroundings, I have had to revise my sense of values. Here, the identification of scat, or animal droppings, becomes of greater importance than the cut of a sport coat. The housekeeping of mountain bluebirds pulls more of my interest than the latest model car does. With the passage of time, I have become possessive of these surroundings. The beautiful mountains have become my old friends.

Chapter One

MOUNTAIN LIVING

Reaction to life in these mountains depends, in large part, on a person's interests and adaptability. I like to regard each day as a picture at an exhibition. Each episode takes its place in the completed picture; every small moment may have its own charm or tragedy. The reaction to these small parts of a day depends on the mood of the viewer. Every event of each day should be acknowledged, not because any one event is of great moment, but because their sum gives the entire day its importance.

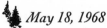 *May 18, 1968*

Today a hodgepodge of small happenings, each taking its place in the unfinished tapestry of springtime. The geese were here at five this morning. They seemed restless and stayed in the meadow only a short time, then flew to the pond behind the cabin. With the usual fanfare they were off a few minutes later, headed for places of greater interest, I suppose.

I see changes in the swallows' nest in the loft of the old barn. The lone egg that has been in the nest all winter is gone now. The cup has a new lining of grass and feathers.

Resinous, balsam-scented buds of cottonwood trees add their heavenly fragrance to this mountain air. The odor of cottonwoods is a fringe benefit of springtime.

A four-point bull elk, covered with a new coat of attractive brown, spent time at the block down meadow. A small doe browsing nearby stopped eating and stared at the bull. He must have sensed that he was being watched because he quickly raised his head. For a time the animals' eyes met, then both returned to their interests of the moment. Later I found eleven deer browsing in the meadow. The four-point elk was back at the block when a small spike bull walked out of the timber. The spike was not allowed at the block until the master had walked to the meadow to graze. This young spike had not completely shed his winter hair. His coat looked ragged and dull.

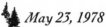 *May 23, 1978*

No wonder the syrup in the hummingbird feeders looked cloudy this morning. The temperature outside is a cool thirty degrees, and there is a breeze. The water in the bird bath is frozen, and at the moment it is snowing. My horse Piccolo is feisty. She was irritated because in her thinking seven-thirty was much too late for the morning feeding. She charged about, throwing her head from side to side in her best "go to hell" manner. As a fitting finale to this display of temper she bucked just before entering the barn. With surprising suddenness, to her at least, her unshod feet slipped and down she went on her bloomin' ass. My unsympathetic hooting hardly helped the situation. She rolled in the mud, picked herself up, and charged into the barn as if she planned an exit through the opposite wall.

Perhaps Piccolo wasn't too far wrong in her attitude. The day has been cold, the ceiling low, there has been thunder and lightning, snow and sleet. Both horses shivered as they ate their afternoon pellets. The dogs, who fear thunder, were unhappy. I couldn't rouse sufficient interest to check the ponds so spent much of the day in jacket and hardhat, peeling rails for fence repair. For a time a flock of gray-crowned rosy finches kept me company. During dinner we had a heavy snowfall and the power failed. Welcome to late May in the mountains!

When it stopped snowing I wandered about in a rain suit, checking ponds. I found little of interest until I arrived at Pond One. Near me at one end of the pond I saw three birds, each a little larger than a gray jay, feeding from the branches of a tree fallen into the water. I saw them through a light mist as they left their perches, flew low over the water, hovered in the air, dipped to the water, then returned. Even through the light fog I could see that these birds were dark above, light below, and had a white band across the tip of their tails. They were most active and seeing them through the fog gave them a ghost-like unreality. Eastern kingbirds in action; a charming performance.

I watch birds and animals at my ponds and know that water is as vital to me as it is to them. Drilling a water well in this mountain valley can be somewhat of a gamble. My own well, established at ninety feet, provided adequate water until the drought of 1967, during which it was pumped dry on two occasions. At my request a group of working geologists tested the area around my cabin with electronic equipment; they reported an excellent water supply at one hundred eighty feet. Their predictions, they said, had proven to be accurate eighty-five percent of the time. On such advice, I decided to drill a new well through the old shaft. The drillers appeared and work was started.

June 7, 1968

Drilling was discontinued today at a depth of two hundred fifteen feet; no new source of water has been found. When it was suggested that we try to re-establish the old well, I agreed. The decision was a good one, but its execution was flawed. When the drillers attempted to pull the pipe to the ninety-foot level, they found the pipe had buckled because of poor welding. When the men tried to pound out this buckling, they broke the pipe. Just dandy! All pulling would thereafter have to be accomplished by traction applied to the inside of the lower segment of the pipe. When this was tried, the pipe didn't move. So to facilitate the operation, they blasted the "drive shoe" at the lower end of the pipe with dynamite. Now, they said, there should be no further trouble. But when they tried pulling the pipe, the cable slipped out of the drill bit, leaving the bit lodged some sixty feet down in the well. Damn!

"Fishing tools" were needed. As the drillers had none, they drove off to find the right equipment. After driving 150 miles, they found no one who would loan them the tools, so returned to try to make their own. The first step, they told me, would be to take an impression of the top of the drill bit. When they attempted this, the heavy impression tray separated from the lowering cable, (again because of a poor weld), dropped, and lodged atop the drill bit. Now they can fish for both the impression tray and the bit.

At that point I decided to go about my business elsewhere, since the efforts thus far depressed me. My notes of the period don't remind me how the tray and bit were retrieved. All I know is that the driller's wife, a very capable woman, came to work with her husband and son for several days.

Somehow the pipe was pulled, the old well re-established. The friendship between the drillers and myself survived. Best of all, the re-established well has proven to be quite satisfactory over the years.

Repairs always seem to cause small dramas. Late in the fall of 1984 a heavy, wet snowfall blanketed, bent and snapped trees over power lines in a wide area of Western Montana. Since the days were mild the real hardship fell on the line men who worked feverishly both night and day to restore power to the homes of we "lodgepole savages." Days later, after the power had been restored and the snow had melted, I began to clean up fallen trees. Near the horse barn in the power line right-of-way, a clump of fifteen-foot trees that had been cut by a line man lay over a pole fence. I assumed that the weight of the trees had broken the fence until the debris was loaded on the pickup leaving the fence exposed. I saw then that the top rail had been neatly sawed in two places. Somehow, instead of being thrown into a fit of temper by this uncalled-for destruction, I chuckled. I pictured the over-worked, frustrated chap who, after cutting through the clump of trees, found a rail fence blocking his passage. He had but three choices of action: walk around, climb over, or saw through that damned rail and step through. He probably didn't ponder long.

Almost as important as power or an adequate supply of fresh water is a satisfactory means of disposing of water once it has been used. This sewage issue seems especially important when the nearest outhouse lies on the far side of a large, snow-filled meadow.

🌲 *January 23, 1969*

Happy morning! I was awake at four, thought it was five, and couldn't go back to sleep. When I flushed the toilet the damned thing wouldn't drain. My next happy discovery was that the thermometer registered ten below.

Later in the morning I borrowed a plunger and a snake. I saw no reason why I shouldn't play plumber. When vigorous use of the plunger in the toilet bowl drained both toilet and washbowl, I sighed with relief. Picking up the tools and leaving the room I made the mistake of looking behind the door into the bathtub. Everything from the toilet now floated merrily about in the tub. Oh, God! Since the plunger did nothing for the tub drain, I tried the snake, which became hopelessly stuck. After a period of bailing, carrying, and a bit of scrubbing, the tub appeared to be virgin clean. I accepted the fact that the drain from the cabin to the septic tank was frozen, probably to remain so for the rest of the winter. Oh well. Pioneers didn't have flush toilets either.

Living in the forest brings great satisfaction in heating with wood, especially when the wood has been cut, hauled, and piled by one's self. But the inherent dangers in burning this wood lower the satisfaction level. I became acutely aware of this in January 1970 when a great roaring in my chimney drove both me and Penny, my elkhound, outside to see what was happening. Flames shot toward the stars, carrying large pieces of flaming pitch that settled back on either the snow-covered roof or the ground. Fortunately I didn't realize that this fire, and a few lesser ones to come, were practice runs.

The real challenge came on November 6, 1977. I knew

that the collection of pitch in my chimney was burning, but since the fire was a slow one and the roof was wet, I wasn't concerned—until I carried my lunch to the table and found smoke billowing out between mantle and fireplace. Somehow, I don't quite remember how, I wrenched the wooden mantle from the stone, doused what flame I could see, and drove to a phone. When my friend Jim arrived, we could see no fire. I connected the hose and stayed near the cabin. The afternoon was uneventful. In the evening I typed in the cabin, walking outside every half hour to check the log wall behind the chimney. I saw nothing unusual; I smelled no smoke. Still, my sleep was uneasy. Twice between ten and two I sat up in bed to look out at the fireplace. Things seemed just fine. Then at two I sat up again and through sleep-filled eyes saw a line of flame above the fireplace. Panic! The dogs hadn't minded; they were accustomed to seeing flames in that part of the cabin. Smoke wasn't yet bad enough to bother. Again I doused what fire I could see and drove to a phone.

Never, I swear, has there been a better crew of firefighters! One man stood outside hosing the smoldering logs, two inside the cabin cut sections of burning logs from the wall with chain saws, a woman in the living room mopped water from the floor, and I tried to remain calm and fit in where needed. I never appreciated the sound of a chain saw until I heard two of them in action in my living room. Afterward the room was a mess but the cabin was still standing and the fire was out. I cleaned the rest of the night and most of the following day. Finally, completely exhausted, *almost* convinced that the fire was really out, and mighty, mighty thankful, I collapsed in bed.

Later, when the burned sections of three logs lay on the ground outside the cabin we could see the cause of the fire. Tile chimney flues had been set against the log wall with only a single layer of glass wool between. The flues had cracked in previous fires, allowing heat to reach the wood.

Not entirely unrelated to the subject of heating with wood is the stove. The old wood-burning stove in my bedroom looked shabby, so in one of my more brilliant decisions I decided to paint it.

 May 3, 1975

Some day I plan to use spray paint properly! This morning I decided to spray the bedroom heater and its chimney. I read the directions on the can, masked with newspaper the areas I thought might catch some of the spray, and spread more newspaper on the oak floor. The actual spraying, I felt certain, should be a cinch. I was barefoot when I started, of course. Before long my feet seemed to be sticking to the papers on the floor. I gave this little thought, finished the spraying, and picked up the papers. I was only mildly surprised when I found slightly darkened floors where the newspapers had not protected them. I was much more surprised when I found black footprints on the floor I'd just walked over. Damn!

I climbed to the loft for the cleaning wax and with it removed all traces of black from the floor. Things looked good again. In doing the waxing, though, I'd waxed myself into a corner. No problem. I walked to the doorway, then turned for a last look. The heater looked fine, but again there were footprints in black on that newly cleaned floor. The wax I'd applied had dissolved some of the paint from the soles of my feet and left new prints . We learn — though some of us learn more slowly than others. With the floor cleaned for the second time, I crawled on hands and knees through the living room and out the door. In the basement I cleaned my feet with gasoline. Directions on the can call for a second spraying. Never again in my house!

Heat and fires go hand in hand outdoors as well as inside. The summer of 1977 was hot and very dry. As the Labor Day holiday drew near many of us were concerned about the possibility of fire in the forest. A journal note shows that worry may, at times, be a wasted effort.

 September 5, 1977

I heard rain on the roof every time I woke during the night. The world is dull and sodden this morning. It is good for the land; to hell with the tourists and the coming holiday. The sky began clearing in mid-afternoon; the evening was lovely. At the osprey nest on the Swan I found an excited young bird perched on a stub above the nest. It called continuously, directing its calls to both an adult perched on a snag nearby and the world at large. For some time the youngster stayed on its perch, then after exercising its wings, it flew to another branch on the same snag. Here it landed with great care. I have the feeling that it hasn't undertaken longer flights yet.

We started back to the pickup. Since the vehicle is only a few weeks old, and since twelve years of driving the old Ford conditioned me for a new love, I take great pride in ownership. Rather than drive a narrow, muddy lane where brush might scratch it, I parked the vehicle on the county road and walked the lane to the nest. As we walked back to the car I tried to keep the dogs from splashing through the puddles, thinking they would track less mud into the cab. I was picking my way over the muddiest portion of the lane when I heard Misty splashing in a puddle behind me. I turned, and in a voice that must have indicated long suffering, told her to get the hell out of the mud. As the dog stood looking up at me, wondering what my problem might be, my feet slipped. I spun into a macabre sort of dance, and with arms waving wildly settled slowly into the mud-filled rut. For a brief moment I lay sprawled in the water, then picked myself up and walked on to the car. The dogs said nothing as we climbed into the cab, but I thought I knew what they might be thinking.

Mud, dirt, and ash are inevitabilities here, as I discovered in 1980.

May 19, 1980

Yesterday, after lunch, we set out on the loop trail around Holland Lake. It was a summer day, bright and pleasant, a day which might have been too warm had it not been for a cooling breeze which came to us from the west. As we crossed the mountain on a trail high above the lake, I noticed a subtle change in the weather. A cloud of dull gray color was blowing in over the Mission Range. By the time we had reached the Jeep our day was overcast. In the evening when I looked toward the west I found that I couldn't see the Missions. I thought, we'll probably have a storm during the night.

As I wandered, half awake, down the trail to the outhouse about five-thirty this morning I was impressed by the unusual appearance of my mountain world. Brush and trees appeared gray in color, roofs were gray and the lily pads on the pond below appeared to be made of concrete. All this I assumed to be a trick of lighting until I started back to the cabin. I saw then that I'd left foot-prints in a thick layer of dust on my way down the trail. Back in the cabin the floors felt sandy to my bare feet. As the light improved I could see large dust particles settling to earth like snowflakes. On the front deck were the tracks of a chipmunk in the dust. My world was a mess!

About noon I drove out to the store. When I asked where all this dust was coming from I was told that I was probably the only person in the entire state of Montana who didn't know that Mount St. Helens had blown her top.

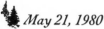 *May 21, 1980*

Yesterday the air cleared so that I was able to see the bare outline of the Swan Range immediately behind the cabin, but was unable to see the Missions across the valley. Today it is stifling; an air pollution emergency has been declared by the governor. Protective surgical masks are being sold on the streets of Missoula. From today's *Missoulian* I learn that "the highest level reached in Missoula County came on Monday evening (May 19) when the air pollution monitor on the courthouse regis-tered an unbelievable 19,228 micrograms, more than thirty times the 625 micrograms level at which local authorities declare a crisis. At the post office today I met a less-than-robust old friend, a protective face mask dangling about her neck and a lighted cigarette in her mouth. She seemed properly horrified that I was maskless, that I wasn't pro-tecting my lungs. Adult reasoning amazes me at times.

Late in the afternoon I heard thunder, then strong gusty winds filled the air with ash. A sudden, intense (though brief) shower left windows frosted with St. Helen's ash, but the grass and lily pads green and normal in appearance. Lilacs near the old barn are blooming profusely; the flowers had opened under their cover of dust and I hadn't noticed.

As I sat in the cabin tonight I saw a brief flash of brilliant color as a male rufous hummingbird flew in and landed on the ground juniper bush beneath the feeder tree. A few moments later when the bird changed its position I saw another flash of brilliant gold. While I was watching the hummer, four deer walked in single file along the shore of the pond behind the cabin. They walked to the mineral block where they licked busily, their ears flapping continuously because of bugs which have somehow managed to survive St. Helens's remains.

Five days later torrential rains caused serious local flooding and banished Mount St. Helens from the headlines. Our problems with the ash seemed to have been settled.

Such grand events are rare, and most of our crises in the Swan are of smaller scale. With animals, for instance—is there a dog anywhere in Montana, other than a house-bound, leash-led animal, that has not at some time tangled with a skunk?

February 10, 1976

Last night Misty tangled with a skunk and as a consequence spent the night alone in her kennel. The entire area between the cabin and the old barn reeked with scent at the time. The odor has now disappeared from the out-of-doors, but the lower floor of the old barn, which is filled with firewood, still smells strongly of skunk. The probable background for this confrontation amuses me. Early in the winter a snowshoe rabbit lived among those woodpiles. I saw the rabbit on several occasions. As I took pleasure in the knowledge that a rabbit had found shelter in the old building, I made certain that there would be pellets in the building for it to eat. Later in the winter, although I saw no fresh rabbit tracks in the snow, my offerings of food continued to disappear at a rapid rate. What I didn't know was that the home of the rabbit had been taken over by a skunk.

Six months later Misty, the Samoyed, had another brush with the skunk. Dawn was just breaking as I sleepily led the horses toward the gate into the lower meadow. I reacted slowly when I saw a rabbit-sized animal as it moved without haste toward the bunkhouse. It hadn't really moved like a rabbit, but suddenly I knew what it was that I had seen! Charlie, Misty's daughter, was at my side and easily controlled, but Misty was missing. I whistled, then heard two choking barks. The dog was still gasping when she came to me from the bunkhouse. Her eyes were closed tightly. She rolled and rubbed her face in the grass, indicating that the skunk had been an excellent marksman. Two pounds of mothballs thrown under the bunkhouse evicted the unwelcome tenant — proving, I suppose, that there are odors even a skunk will not tolerate.

Another animal pest is the wood rat, the only North American animal that is interested in bringing home useless objects. Known in the West as the "pack rat," it is the original curio collector. To me the pack rat is an attractive little guy, soft-furred with large hairy ears and a furred tail. In a live trap the pack rat usually sits quietly, looking up at its captor with large, black, inquiring eyes. I once found a pack rat nest on top of a woodpile in the old barn. It had been used for a month or two, yet was spotlessly clean. Constructed of soft materials from various sources, it was built in the form of an igloo with a high-domed roof and a round doorway. Like the dwellings of some humans I know, the house was clean because all litter had been thrown outside. The nest itself had no odor, but chunks of wood near it smelled strongly of urine and feces It is this characteristic smell that makes the pack rat such an objectionable tenant.

I had not seen many of these little beasts until the winter of 1976-1977 when, for some reason, their numbers in the loft of my horse barn increased to near epidemic proportions. In late January, as I released the eleventh pack rat of the winter about a mile from the cabin, I began to wonder if pack rats, like homing pigeons, head for home when liberated. When on January 25 Misty informed me by her actions that we again had a visitor in the barn loft, I raised the trap and placed a dab of orange-colored enamel on the undersurface of the rat's furry tail before driving to the release point. For the next twenty-three days the live trap sat open and waiting; on the twenty-fourth day I found the trap closed and a pack rat patiently waiting for release. When I lifted the trap and looked up from below, I found the telltale orange spot on the animal's tail. I had spent much of the winter catching and liberating the same animal. It had taken this chap twenty-four days to return through the soft, deep snow, but return it did. As it ran from the trap into the timber, this time seven miles from home, I wondered what the homing instinct would do for it now.

Another of the same species became a star performer again in 1987. The severed tops of clematis vines alerted me to the possible presence of a pack rat in the old barn. The next morning I found the animal in a live trap in the loft, patiently waiting for liberation—or so I thought. Since I had learned that pack rats return when released too close to home, I drove for five miles along a winding mountain road, then opened the trap at the roadside expecting the animal to disappear in the brush. Instead, it surprised me by scurrying across the road and disappearing under the pickup. To be certain it had climbed the bank there, I lifted the hood, carefully checked engine and frame, and crawled under the vehicle to check from below. I confess to feeling smug as I parked in front of the cabin. However, when I found Frosty sitting near the front wheel, looking up at the hood and listening, I began to wonder. Up again went the hood. This time I saw a small foot protruding from a blind pocket in the metal frame. Damn! My uninvited guest had hitched a ride back home. We tumbled into the vehicle and drove off. This time when I stopped and prepared to prod the stowaway from its hiding place, my passenger was gone. I suspected that I had been outwitted. Where had it given me the slip? Back at the cabin I reset the trap in the loft and placed one in the basement-garage. The next morning a demure pack rat waited in the basement trap. When I released it in the timber, eight miles from home and well away from the vehicle, its expression, if I read it correctly, was one of great disappointment.

I found a more welcome squatter one day in April when checking birdhouses. I had been disappointed that the duck house placed in a tree on the shore of Pond Five had never housed a nesting goldeneye. The preceding fall I had found the house filled with grass and had removed it; now grass could be seen in the doorway again. I nailed some aluminum sheeting around the trunk of the tree, then raised the ladder to the house for a cleaning.

The first handful of grass came out easily. I reached in the house a second time, clutched a fistful of grass and started to pull. This time I met with more resistance. Immediately behind the grass the head and body of a small squirrel appeared in the doorway. The animal hesitated there for a brief moment; then leaped. As I watched from above a membrane connecting the front with the rear legs grew taut. This membrane seemed to serve as a glider as the small animal sailed downward, at an angle, to the base of a tree nearby. It rapidly climbed the tree where it sat looking down at me.

I now found myself with a job half done. I had evicted a flying squirrel whose appearance delighted me. I'd already nailed a wide band of metal about the trunk of the nesting tree so that no animal could climb to the house again. I felt that I must make retribution and that I must do it quickly. Back at the cabin I enlarged the doorway of a new bluebird house, then hurried back to hang it on a tree near the duck house. Not until this was done did I remove the rest of the grass from the duck house, collect my tools, and return to the cabin.

Both the creatures and the mountain environment are often sources of joy. I recall a winter walk in 1987 when the snow cover, although days old, looked fresh and white. I came upon an area of dazzling, "hairy" snow at the side of the mountain road. The long hairs had been formed by slow thawing, refreezing, and frost. Scattered among the "hairs" were crystals of a great size, all standing on end. Most of these crystals reflected a pale blue light, but there were reds and greens as well. Nearby snow was crusted with large, flat crystals, all huge, sparkling diamonds. Later, as I walked through the timber on my way back to the cabin, I found more reason to loiter. In a patch of sunlight were three glittering frost flowers. Each blossom, a little larger than a quarter, had formed on the blunt, deer-browsed end of a three-pronged serviceberry branch. Each flower had four petals; each petal was a large, flat ice crystal. Perfect symmetry.

In mid-March of the same year, another day started bright and cool, but by seven a light fog had moved in. I stood in the loft, about to throw hay to Piccolo, when the silence was broken by the loud honking of Canada geese. I waited as four geese in formation dropped to eye level in front of the open door then sailed in an arc that took them to the pond down meadow. A splash, then silence. Snow fell much of the afternoon, its large, wet flakes clinging to everything they touched. It was still snowing at dusk, large fuzz that looked like cotton. Eight inches waited on the ground at bedtime. Beautiful!

Still later in the year, after three days of dullness and rain, the early-morning sun backlit the hummingbird feeder, the globe of which glowed like a lighted bulb. Hummers swarming about it scattered when a colorful western tanager flew in and landed on a branch above them, sending down a shower of glistening raindrops. The tanager then dropped to what was probably his first feeding of the day. Droplets sparkled on trees and brush, mist rose in a cloud from the pond below, and peaks in both ranges wore a thin cap of fresh snow. Both dogs, their coats wet from explorations in the brush, lay on the grass in the sunlight. Piccolo grazed contentedly in the meadow. I heard no sounds other than hummingbird wings, bird song, and the blowing of a distant deer. I decided it was a fine day to be alive in the mountains.

Many lesser events fit into the mosaic of my life in these hills. One gray dawn Piccolo stood in the meadow, shoulders slumped, head down, obviously dozing. She was oblivious to the small doe which stood before her, looking up into her face. A doe and her two fawns of last season didn't see me until I was almost upon them. They ran slowly, mother flanked on each side by a child. Three white flags waved as if synchronized, three sets of hooves in step all the way.

Two earthquake shocks in 1987 seemd tame beside the tawny beast that I saw disappearing at the corner of the cabin a few evenings later. Hurrying back in the direction from which it had come, it had seen me before I had seen it. Piccolo snorted and ran about the meadow; she, too, had spotted the animal — and hadn't liked what she had seen. My final glimpse as the animal disappeared around a bend in the game trail showed muscular hindquarters carrying a long, upturned tail that ended in a tip of deep brown. It is reasonable to assume that the head of this beast was that of a mountain lion, too.

All the life here excites me, none more than the returning birds whose daily work of food-finding makes a scene of perpetual beauty. As they come back to my feeder each year, I measure my seasons in this place by the sound of their wings.

July, 22, 1987

When the hummingbirds returned after their scheduled absence this summer, some of them again staked claim to the feeder that hangs on the front wall of the outhouse. There, the overhanging roof together with the projecting log walls on each side intensify the sound of hovering wings for anyone in the building. This afternoon I looked out over the pond at the wooded slopes and peaks in the Swan Range. A few hummers hovered over the water below, then darted after insects, intent on obtaining their protein requirements for the day. The doorway through which I watched, framed by profusely blooming tuberous begonias, formed a perfect setting for the fighting, chasing, playing birds as they zoomed across the opening in their travels to and from the feeder.

Chapter Two

THE LANDSCAPE

The best cure I know for the depression that sometimes follows long periods of dullness and rain is reading journal entries written in years of drought. When the country is tinder dry, it gives scant comfort to be told that there hasn't been a fire of consequence in this valley since the 1920s. My first experience with bitter drought here was in 1967. For a time that summer the entire forest was closed to travel except for those of us who had homes there.

 *September 6, 1967*

Yesterday was a worrisome day. The afternnon temperature was 104 degrees. The sky clouded in mid-afternoon and there was some wind. It seems odd to know there can't be rain if the sun shines, yet to be afraid if clouds form.

Early this morning I lay in bed listening to the rain as it ran off the roof onto the deck. Beautiful, beautiful music! Later, I learned that eight fires had been started by lightning, none of them in this immediate area.

Six years later the dryness of the country commanded greater space in my journal.

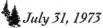

July 31, 1973

We started our climb to Rumble Lake on the west slope of the Swan Range in the cool of the morning. The greatest attraction of lower Rumble Lake is the beauty of twin falls at its inlet. But today one of the twins was completely dry; the other a mere trickle. The upper falls were no more impressive. Nothing about the scene offered any stimulation for this hiker.

We climbed a bit, but since I was having no fun and Misty was just following, it wasn't long before we were on our way back down the mountain. At one of our stops I noticed that the dog sitting near me raised first one front paw, then the other. When I placed my hand on the rock on which she rested, I found it too hot to tolerate. Finally back on the foothills trail we drank greedily from Rumble Creek. While my friend walked belly-deep in the cold water, I soaked my shirt, then put it back on my body, dripping wet. We agree, I think, that it would be well for us to stay off the mountain until we have rain.

In the middle of August that year three fires a few miles north of the Swan Valley caused both excitement and worry. Two fires on national forest land were quickly controlled, but the third, the Goat Creek fire on state land, blew up on the night of the August 16 and the Forest Service was asked to take over management of the blaze. For the next few days planes carrying fire retardant from headquarters in Missoula flew over my cabin. Two boxcar-sized helicopters arrived and spent their time dipping water from a lake and dumping it on the flaming forest. For a time both mountain ranges were obscured by smoke. On the eighteenth of the month all forests were closed to entry. It was said to be the most difficult year of the century thus far for Glacier Park's dwindling glaciers. Newspaper headlines screamed that nine thousand men were combating western forest fires.

My own attitude at that time shows in my notes.

August 19, 1973

There is little incentive to work these days. It is unsafe to work in the timber with a chain saw, one doesn't dare drive in the timber to load previously cut firewood, and it is too dusty to clean the cabin or to wash the windows. Just the sight of our ailing countryside discourages work!

August 29, 1973

My day started badly. Yesterday I learned that the Forest Service has yielded to outfitter pressure and opened the Bob Marshall wilderness and its three valley approaches to travel by permit. Damn! With one of the approaches on the mountain directly behind my cabin and the country explosively dry, I could be burned out here before anyone could hope to stop a fire. I am furious! This morning I stomped into the ranger station and announced that since the Bob has now been fireproofed, I'd like a permit for travel. The chap on duty who knew me well naturally told me to try and get it. I exploded, pouring my hostility toward a spineless Forest Service upon a startled audience. It was a cheap display of temper, and the fact that I knew it made me madder still. The fellows in the station hadn't made the decision; they were merely following orders given by desk-bound chiefs in Kalispell.

I took the permit and seethed most of the way up the

mountain to old Holland Lookout. High on the trail, I stopped to watch a hawk soaring below me on an updraft. The bird rose slowly in wide circles without moving a wing. As it passed directly over me I saw it staring down at us. When it was gone I suddenly realized that the mountains were working their magic; I was slowly beginning to relax. It was almost uncomfortably cool on the peak, but the sky was very blue with white clouds of attractive shapes and the view of wilderness enhanced by haze. As I sat eating, a female tanager flew in, snatched an insect from a rock, and was off again without a sound. I glassed the Missions. Suddenly I realized that I was seeing a small lake below Mountaineer Peak, a lake I'd never seen from this spot before. The water in its center was free of ice but there was either ice or snow about its edges. When we started moving again we dropped into the Bob and explored the rocky-shored lakes in the Necklace chain. I was tired when I arrived home, physically weary but mentally at peace.

The next day, with the country still explosively dry and a holiday coming up, the forest supervisor opened the entire forest to travel. Fortunately, the weather forecast was in error. There was a light rain during the night, enough to wet the surface, and it was still misting lightly when I woke in the morning. No peaks were visible in either range. The scene was pleasantly unpleasant! The horses rolled and were covered with mud. I'd forgotten just how beautiful mud could look on a white horse. Later, when I walked to the barn to give the horses their pellets, I was astonished to see new snow on the peaks in both ranges. The cabin was uncomfortably cool but I refused to start a fire.

Both 1977 and 1979 were such dry years that young birds starved in some of the houses because insects were in short supply. There were fewer insects because of spring's long periods of dullness and cold, and summer's intense heat and dryness. About the middle of August of 1979, when things seemed hopeless, we had a reprieve.

August 13, 1979

The drumming of rain on the roof in the afternoon was sweet music. The dogs who haven't heard this sound for such a long time were intimidated by it. It was a token shower, of short duration. But there was enough moisture to leave puddles in the roadway that were welcomed by bathing birds. The greatest benefit of this shower has been psychological. We now know that it is possible for rain to fall!

After several showers washed the thick coating of dust from the trees and brush, the country looked fresh and green again. The morning of August 23 started clear, bright, and pleasantly cool. It felt good to be moving in the high country again.

August 23, 1979

Everything went well until I left the trail and with the dogs started to climb toward the saddle above. I'd misjudged the terrain and soon found myself stumbling over rocks that were hidden by bear grass and flowers or trying to avoid hidden holes where a misstep could ruin an ankle. Finally I'd had enough; we climbed back to the trail. As I sat eating lunch, storm clouds appeared in the western sky. This seemed to be no time to climb higher so we headed for home. By the time we reached the large lake we'd passed in the morning we were blown along by high winds. I could see lightning behind us and could hear thunder. On the lower switchbacks we walked through light rain mixed with hail. We traveled our last mile at a trot with lightning crashing into the mountains around us. As we climbed into the Jeep it started to pour.

The unpleasantness of a searing, dry summer tends to magnify delight in more pleasant weather that follows.

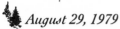 *August 29, 1979*

A colorful evening sky, a fitting ending for a day of such beauty. Most of the color tonight was in the sky's bowl. Cloud formations and streaks in the southern sky took on a bright pink color. Above me in the bowl of the sky and extending far to the north, both clouds and streaking were a brilliant orange-flame. The orange changed slowly to a subdued salmon, which was outlined in many of the formations by a dull lavender. A silver moon peeked through. At the height of the display I heard a coyote singing, far to the north.

As if to compensate for the month before, the entire month of September that year was warm and bright. Beautiful Indian summer days were much too short for long jaunts into the hills but perfect for working about the home place. Rain dropped in quantities sufficient to restore beauty to the mountainsides, but not enough to allow for the safe burning of logging slash. Consequently we were treated to lovely fall weather without the smoke that fall usually brings. Some sunsets were spectacular. I remember one particularly: dull lavender clouds in the south slowly took on a bright pink hue, and at the same time the western sky over the Mission Range changed, first to bright gold, then to salmon, finally to brilliant flame. The colors lingered. There were no sounds.

Some of the summer electrical storms that pass over these mountains bring no rain. Mid-August of 1981, when the temperature climbed day after day, smoke drifted down to us from large fires in Canada. Oddly, the grass and brush were still relatively green here, belying the severe dryness. At about noon on August 25, as I crossed the sunlit meadow with the sickle-bar mower, an earsplitting crash made me flinch. This crash was followed by the loud rumble of thunder. The sky was clear except for a few cumulous clouds in its vault. This bolt out of the blue started a fire in the timber less than a mile from the cabin. Fortunately the blaze was located quickly and extinguished. For the next few nights we were bombarded by dry electrical storms that left us with thirty-five fires at Condon and more throughout western Montana.

This was a worrisome time. The valley hosted two large fire camps, helicopters carried men and supplies about the area, liquid retardant was dropped from large planes, and small crews spread out to take care of smaller smokes. A temporary landing spot for 'copters on the mountains above Holland Lake, five miles south of my cabin, was hastily evacuated when flames suddenly raced up toward it. Two days later I hiked the Holland Canyon trail where I had a close-up view of the still-burning area. A mop-up crew was busy on the mountain and as I watched, 'copters dropped retardant on still burning areas that were inaccessible to men on the ground. I was amazed at the accuracy of these drops.

With cooler nights and a few slight rains, the air activity over the valley gradually ceased; the fire season of 1981 finally ended.

Under certain conditions, this mountain country can depress and worry a person. But at other times it has a magical ability to soothe and restore mental peace. Peace of mind — that quality in life which many seek and so few find — is something money can't buy. Peace may be the result of a sunrise or a beautiful sunset. It may spring from a grand vista; it may be found in a tiny nook. It may be great music, a good book, or the sight of a newborn fawn. Or it may be none of these things. Peace for one individual may be sheer boredom for another.

Rereading my journal notes brings many small, peaceful happenings back to me with great clarity. The dates are not as important as the events themselves.

—About ten tonight I walked out of the cabin for a last look about. Two deer on the shore of the pond behind the cabin looked up at me. I stood quietly until they had gone back to the mineral block, then walked to the front of the cabin where my friend Penny, the elkhound, was sleeping. Brilliant colors over the Mission Range formed a proper background for two ducks flying in from somewhere. The pair made three wide circles in the colorful sky, then headed north and out of the picture. I heard splashing down meadow as playing deer ran in and out of the pond. With binoculars I could see seven vague figures at play, and another standing quietly at the block. A deer blew in the timber near me. Swainson's thrushes, whose melodious songs characteristically spiral upward, sang in full chorus to the beauty of the evening.

— Frequent showers during the day have set the stage for a rainbow against the Swan Range. The peaks are hidden by a dense overcast sky. Only the barest outlines of the lower, wooded slopes can be seen. The lower arch of this double rainbow is unusually bright, its colors vivid and well defined. The upper arch, also bright, is most brilliant at either end. Between the upper and the lower arches are mottled colors—blues, reds, and violets. The entire area below the lower arch is an opaque, bright silver. I leaned against the old barn, watching this unique display until all the color had faded.

— Oh, for the ability to adequately describe the sunset over the Mission Range tonight! Initially the colors involved only a small portion of the western sky. Dull blue-gray clouds were dramatically edged by brilliant yellow. Very slowly the colors spread, finally involving the sky over the entire range. Between the clouds and the peaks below them were a variety of colors—orange, flame, salmon, and red. Streaks of red extended out into the sky from those areas which were most vivid. I stood watching as the colors lingered, ignoring the nickering of the horses as they tried to remind me they had not yet had their nightly pellets.

— Some mornings are created just to be seen! At six I found four deer at the block behind the cabin. All were reflected in the quiet water of the pond. A cow elk grazed in the meadow. As I rounded the corner of the cabin on my way to the barn I was stopped by the sky over the Mission Range. In this somber sky a faint rainbow extended in its arch over most of the range. Gradually the colors became brighter and a double leg developed in the north. The colors in the rainbow became more bril-

liant, then slowly began to fade. Then a redwing black-
bird in the top of a ponderosa near me began to sing in
muted tones, as if it too realized that this was no time for
exuberance.

On a bright afternoon late in the summer when I was
wandering off-trail between ponds, I came upon a well-pre-
served, ancient stump that was light gray and about hip high.
The upper surface of this stump gave the appearance of
craggy mountains separated by narrow valleys. Green moss
grew in most of the valleys, and bunchberry plants grew in
the moss. Most of these bore clusters of bright, orange-red
berries. When I came upon the stump for the first time it
stood in full sunlight, a thing of exquisite beauty.

Late in the month of June, one of the small ponds near
my cabin was covered with a coating of pollen, which left its
surface dull and unattractive. But on my rounds one evening,
this tree-surrounded pothole provided me with one of those
unbelievably beautiful surprises that make life worth living.
I arrived at the pond about an hour before sundown. Since
the sun was low in the west; its rays reached the water's surface at an angle. I was still high on the east ridge when I first
sighted the effect this had on the water. The pollen-covered
surface glowed with subtle colors — deep reds, pinks, salmons,
oranges, yellows and various shades of both blue and green.
For the most part these colors lay in wide bands across the
pond from one shore to the other. From a distance, the surface seemed to swirl where one color gently faded into another. For some time I stood with my eyes fixed on the beauty
below. When finally the sun sank behind the Mission Range,

I reluctantly came down off the ridge, followed by three patient dogs. As we moved toward the water, the colors became less marked. When we stood on shore, the pollen-covered water was again dirty gray.

Checking ponds early one morning in July, I walked the east shore of the large pond rather than the west where I usually travel. That day I had located all members of the goldeneye family, had glassed the water's surface for other occupants, then had moved on. The sun was still low in the eastern sky; its rays, when they penetrated the canopy at all, reached the forest floor on a slant. I climbed over downed trees and glanced up into the forest. There, surrounded by the darkened forest, stood a single bush of some size, which, lit by a beam of sunlight, gleamed as if it were made of highly polished silver. I stood still in awe, forgetting that I had other things to do, even forgetting young Frosty who waited patiently at my side. Slowly, I moved up the ridge toward the brightly gleaming object. As I came closer, the shine became more subdued, and when I examined the leaves closely they were the same dull silver-green as were the leaves on the bushes around it. Back at my original position, the bush gleamed again, a shrub from fantasy-land. For many days I walked the same route at about the same time of day and saw the same picture. The shrub has a name, of course: the silver buffalo berry.

Over the years I've reaped other rewards for slowing the daily pace. Once, early in the summer, I discovered an extensive patch of rare mountain lady's slipper orchids in a low area not far from my cabin. I examined a flower closely to convince myself it was real. I'd not discovered them before, I suppose, because I'd taken quicker routes and hadn't walked at the time the lovely plants bloomed.

In spite of cold and struggles with snow, ice, and firewood, winter also has offered many moments of great beauty, of peace and of relaxation, as my journal shows.

—When I walked to the barn this morning just before sunrise, the snow-covered trees were still lit by the beautiful moon. A mauve sky above the Missions served as a background for peaks of ivory. Frost sparkled on all surfaces that were not covered with snow.

—We had fresh snow yesterday, and although the morning is a cool four below zero, this day is a lovely as any we've had all winter. When the dogs and I left the cabin on the cross-country webs this afternoon the temperature had risen to twenty above. The blue Montana sky and the stark, white, sunlit peaks with timbered slopes below presented a picture of unbelievable beauty. Cumulous clouds played about the peaks as if they enjoyed being there. We climbed along a softly singing creek where we found the tracks of a lone elk. On a high logging road we saw deer tracks, made as the animals browsed the brush at the roadside. Superimposed on these tracks were the prints of coyotes that had trotted leisurely down the road, stopping to sniff here, digging there. Now we've added our own tracks to this pattern in the snow.

—When we left the cabin tonight the temperature was zero. A full moon, traveling in a blue, star-studded sky, lit my world. Prominent white peaks in both ranges added their beauty to the scene. I heard no sounds other than the crunching of boots on snow. Our pace was slow, our walk filled with peace and the beauty of the evening. With just a little imagination I could picture this as the perfect setting for elves and fairies I learned about in early childhood.

— At seven this evening the temperature was zero, the air was still, the moon full, and there were brightly sparkling stars in the sky. Rough spots on the surface of the pond ice must have been free of snow covering. I saw three brilliantly shining points of light on the pond's surface, lines of light radiating from each central area of brightness. Near me, common snow-covered lodgepoles drooped under their loads. But those across the pond and on the slopes formed a delicate fretwork of lights and darks which led my eyes up the mountain to the moonlit peaks above. I forgot both time and temperature as I stood quietly, listening to the silence.

These surroundings can bring peace or excitement. Thoughts of the high country invariably stir within me feelings of eager anticipation. In my early years of travel here, I went as a follower; later I preferred traveling alone, as an explorer. A lone traveler has added risks, but I've been careful and lucky. When uninitiated visitors ask about hiking in this country, they invariably ask about distances. They do not realize that in these mountains it is terrain, rather than distance, that is the more important factor.

I need nothing to jog my memory of my first long day hike in the Mission Mountains on July 28, 1969. My friend Cal, the wilderness ranger, and I left the trailhead before daybreak. We were in the hills for a total of thirteen hours, on our feet and moving for at least twelve. Our route took us across two high saddles, one of them twice. When we dropped

from the first saddle into the Post Creek drainage of the Flathead Indian Reservation, I was in country I'd never seen
before.

The views were breathtaking as we moved down the
mountain. Three sparkling lakes lay below us, and
MacDonald Peak, the highest point in the Missions, lay directly across the drainage still wearing its mantle of winter
snow. For a few moments we stood on the shore of Cliff Lake,
a jewel bordered on two sides by cliffs and peaks, then forded
its fast-flowing outlet and were on our way. Since fish had
not yet been planted in Cliff Lake, we saw no fire circles and
found no litter. There were no "people trails" in the entire
drainage.

In some areas we moved through extensive beds of
brightly colored alpine flowers; in others our feet sank into
luxuriant growths of moss or grass. We hiked along a roaring creek and passed a sheer cliff where a full stream of water fell to the valley floor from Lake-of-the-Clouds, nestled
in its cirque high above us. Water from snowmelt cascaded
down the mountainside in many places, softly roaring in its
eagerness to join the madly moving creek beside us. We were
walking through grizzly country. At Iceflow Lake, high in
the drainage, we sat for the first time, soaking our tired feet
in this tiny lake on the surface of which chunks of winter ice
still floated.

As I unlaced my boots I thought with pleasure of the lunch
I carried in my day pack. I was famished! With my feet in
the water and my rear resting comfortably on a flat rock, I
reached in the day pack. To my horror I found that in my
haste that morning I'd grabbed a sack of unripe plums in-

stead of my carefully bagged lunch. Good planning by this would-be mountain man! Still, I didn't do too badly. My generous friend shared his sandwich, and the stock of dried food which we both normally carry in our packs helped, too. After lunch we continued to climb to the Ashley saddle. There I waited, snapping pictures while Cal dodged around the corner to pick up an exposed film he had left on the mountain a few days before. Fifteen minutes later we were glissading down a snowfield on our return journey.

Other mountain trips have been just as memorable. In August of 1970, with reluctance, I started on a high trip through the southern Missions with my friend Jim. We had had many days of dull, wet weather and the long-range forecast was for four more days of possible showers. Unknown high mountain country is a poor place to be when the sky is dull and rock surfaces are slippery. We walked through light rain that first afternoon and somewhat glumly made camp at the outlet of Graywolf Lake. But our spirits rose with the sun the next morning. We broke camp after a good breakfast, then started on a long contour of the east side of Graywolf. We were but a short distance from the end of the lake when I stepped from a wet bear grass slope to a rock slide, slipped down between two rocks, and knew that my trip was over. God, how that ankle hurt! I hobbled across the slide, removed boot and sock, then soaked my deformed ankle in the cold lake. The next morning, with an ankle twice its normal size, I tried to make it back to the outlet. I didn't get far; there was nothing to do but wait for help. That longed-for wilderness challenge had been my undoing; now I would have time to enjoy its solitude.

With never a word about his ruined trip, Jim grabbed a day pack, told me not to expect help until the following morning, and left on his long trip out to the phone. Penny, the elkhound, who knew Jim well and loved him, refused to leave me. Surprisingly my day was almost a delight. The ankle pained me, of course, but with slow and careful hobbling I was able to climb the slabs above camp. There I spent most of my day looking out over the lake, with Penny at my side. Graywolf is a large, beautiful lake, much longer than it is wide, with an irregular shoreline. It is surrounded by mountain peaks and cliffs, bear grass tufts, and timber. The day was bright and cool. As the sun moved in its orbit, the reflections of the peaks in the quiet water moved, too. Occasionally these near-perfect reflections of the surrounding mountains were distorted, or wiped out, when breezes brought sparkling ripples to the surface of the water. Directly below me, in a patch of green, the large, white flowers of bear grass added to this lovely scene.

I had finished my evening meal, washed my dishes, and limped back up the slabs to enjoy the quiet of evening when I heard the clatter of a distant helicopter. Steadily the drone became louder. Damn! I thought. The peace of the evening was ruined for me, at least until the 'copter passed over the lake and went on its way. It didn't occur to me that this mechanical monster might be coming for me — until it circled, flew in over the mountain, and prepared to land. The pilot helped me break camp, load the gear, and get into the bubble, then handed the apprehensive dog to me. Penny struggled in my arms. She fought harder when the door closed and was almost manic when the motor started. But as we began to move she became a perfect tourist. She sat quietly in my lap, looking to one side at the scenery, then to the other.

As I climbed from the helicopter at the Forest Service airstrip, the lanky, redheaded dispatcher stalked across the road to the field, a shotgun cradled in his arms and a mean look in his eyes. His comment was, "Well, they shoot horses, don't they?" I limped to the waiting vehicle knowing that I would be doing no more hiking for some time.

I had won, yet I had lost. The next day as the orthopedist taped my ankle he told me that not only had I had a bad sprain, but that I had dislocated a tendon as well. I'm glad that I didn't know then that the ankle would be troublesome over a three-year period. Because of my slowness the next year, I hiked alone. The sprain would be responsible, in part, for my learning to be self-reliant on my high-country rambles.

The Swans have also offered me great hiking opportunities.

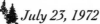 *July 23, 1972*

This was a day of sunshine and frolic. Our rambles took us to a high basin in the Swans where young Misty, the Samoyed, careened down mountainsides on crusted snow, obviously having the time of her life. When my own footing seemed less than secure, this new friend came to me with a large stick in her mouth and banged it against my legs, daring me to try to take it from her. This was also a day of flowers. At lower elevations we found alpine buttercups everywhere, glacier lilies in profusion, and isolated masses of forget-me-nots. Now, at dusk, a delightful weariness takes over this body of mine. I sit watching a large bull elk as he walks down the hill to the block across the pond behind the cabin. The giant is followed by a smaller bull. For a time both lick quietly, then the smaller animal is nudged from the block. He is not allowed to return.

July 26, 1972

Today we enjoyed more off-trail travel, this time in a high basin in the Mission Range. The terrain here was mostly bear grass and rocks, but we did find alpine flowers blooming in profusion in the wetter areas. There were alpine buttercups, glacier lilies, delicate shooting stars, even wild onions in bloom. Snowmelt cascaded down the mountainside in many places. Our climb had taken us from summer back into spring. Both Misty and I love these high places; we take on new life when we wander about in them.

I had no problems in the basin where rocks, hidden by bear grass, can be treacherous. But back on the trail as we barreled down the mountain toward the trailhead, my toe caught on a tree root and I landed on my silly face. No problem; I'd just learned my lesson in humility for the day.

About two weeks afterward, Misty and I were back in that same drainage. This time we stayed high in the basin, eventually climbing its north rim. I stood on the crest, enjoying views that I'd not seen from this location before. Both Cold and Frigid lakes lay below us. This proved to be an excellent spot from which to view the portion of the Mission divide, which separates the main Cold drainage from reservation lands to the west. This section of the divide is impressive—massive, rugged, and formidable. Immediately below it to the west lies Terrace Lake, a small hole almost completely surrounded by cliffs and peaks. The lake still sported a snowfield along one shore; ice still floated on its surface.

It was cold and windy on the crest. When I decided that I had had my fill of distance scenery, Misty and I dropped down the south slope. Here we enjoyed protection from the wind and were able to eat in relative comfort. Slowly I became conscious of an unusual sound approaching from the northwest. From my protected lunch spot I could see nothing, but the noise was obviously manmade and flying at a low altitude over the wilderness area. I fumed. I didn't climb for a better view but sat pouting behind my rock, hoping the damned thing would go away. Later, when I returned to the valley floor, I was asked if I had seen the low-flying meteor. Folks in the valley had seen it, other hikers had seen it, newspapers carried stories about it, but I hadn't missed a mouthful as I impatiently waited for the return of peace and quiet.

 *August 17, 1972*

We walked down a high scree slope beside cliffs covered with brightly colored lichen. The scree on which we walked appeared to be worn, giving me the feeling that this route had been used before. A little lower on the mountain we skirted a large boulder then turned down a hogback between two drainages. Here our route became a well-used trail.

When I rounded a bend I found a large mule deer buck, wearing a magnificent rack, standing in the trail ahead of me. This majestic animal was as startled by my sudden appearance as I was surprised to see him. My reaction was to hold my breath and freeze in position; his was to leap from the trail and disappear among the large boulders at the trailside.

Much lower on the mountain, as we walked along an

old skid road, I found young Misty standing with her nose only inches from a porcupine. A shout distracted the dog long enough for me to grab her. With apparent indifference the quilled warrior then climbed a tree. Still farther down the skid road I saw my small, white friend running up the mountainside behind a large black bear. Although the dog must have regarded me as a spoilsport, she did give up the chase and came to my whistle.

I may have grown too fond of these lovely mountains, since each new fire circle, each tree scarred by a careless camper, and each bit of litter seems like a personal insult. One cool, bright morning in late July, I left the trailhead with Misty, headed for the Hemlock-Elk saddle in the Missions. At the inlet of Hemlock Lake we stopped for a moment to watch a dipper, a bird that was much too preoccupied to pass the time of day. In the lower basin, Misty dropped to the tiny creek and spooked a mule deer drinking there. In the upper basin we found flowers that were still fresh and lovely. I was eagerly anticipating the last bit of climbing; the trail winds upward through low cliffs then suddenly breaks out into the open on the saddle to a view that I love so much.

I suppose that the brightness of the day, the beauty of the flowers, and the satisfaction of making the climb itself had left me unprepared for the intrusion of what some regard as the "real world." In that last short climb the trail curved around a huge boulder. I looked up and there on a flat rock surface was graffiti in silver paint. What a hell of a thing to do! I fumed for a time — then off came the day pack. Using the abrasive surface of broken rocks that I found on the trail, I scraped as much paint from the flat rock wall as I could. I stayed on the saddle for some time, feeling the anger dissipate as I looked out over the lovely drainage.

After lunch, when relaxation became so complete that I thought I must either move or sleep, we started down. At one point on the high trail, I turned and looked into the eyes of a smiling white dog. She stood on a rock above me, perfectly framed by colorful flowers. Back in the lower basin I stopped to examine recent bear droppings on the trail. Misty waited behind me for a time, then brushed my hand as she trotted around me. Concentrating as I was on the freshness of the bear poop, this sudden contact of hand with animal hair meant only one thing—bear! I jumped.

Several days later with a can of paint remover and a wire brush in the day pack, I climbed again to the Hemlock-Elk saddle. At the small lake above Hemlock I stopped to watch tadpoles the size of quarters, lolling about in the shallow water near shore. There must have been two hundred of them in the company of a few large frogs. Finally, the graffiti completely removed, the rock face still wet but otherwise normal in appearance, we climbed on to the saddle. The satisfaction of a job done was not my only reward for the day. The view to the west was especially lovely, the sky was very blue, and in it floated cumulous clouds. Elk and Spook lakes nestled below their cliffs across the drainage as if there was no place in the world they would rather be. There was a pleasant breeze and the light showed varicolored lichen on the rocks around me. Three solitary vireos kept me company for a time, then a family of mountain bluebirds flew in and perched near me on low snags. There were no discordant notes on our trip back down the mountain. I was weary but pleased with life as we climbed into the Jeep.

I had been grounded toward the end of the hiking season of 1974 because of a five-day elk-hunting season. On the day after the shooting ended I grabbed the day pack and headed for the hills with Misty. We lunched on the Mission divide, overlooking the Post Creek drainage in the Flathead Indian Reservation. It was cold on the divide, cold enough for a heavy wool shirt and a Windbreaker. After lunch, Misty wandered off on a mission of her own. I was storing memories for the winter dream bank when a patch of white on the divide below me caught my eye. Misty! How the hell did she get down there? But when I looked about I found the white dog not far from me, curled up asleep beneath a juniper bush. With binoculars I could see the spot of white below me on the divide was a mountain goat. It must have walked out from behind a boulder shortly before I noticed it. The animal stood quietly, posing as an artist might wish to paint it. It stared across the drainage at a goat that was moving about on the mountain below MacDonald Peak. Finally this white neighbor walked to the base of what appeared to be an almost vertical cliff, climbed it with ease, and disappeared from view.

Such interruptions are always welcome. Others I regret.

August 11, 1975

Hiking today has been a mixed bag! The morning was delightful. The hiking itself went well both on- and off-trail, at a good speed and without fatigue. We lunched on Point St. Charles. Turquoise Lake, immediately below, is a gem nestled among peaks and cliffs. Lake-of-the-Clouds as seen through Lone Tree Pass was open, but ice still

floated on its surface. Those rugged peaks in the southern Missions stood stark and clear; I've never seen them
more lovely. To the east the beauty of the Swan Range
and Valley told me again how fortunate I am to live here.
Lunch eaten, spiritually satiated, and at peace with my
world, I decided to drop to Turquoise for a drink of water before starting the long trek out to the trailhead. It
was at that point that my day began to fall apart!

My drop down the mountain was pleasant enough
until I started moving down the lower slabs toward the
outlet of the lake. I glanced up, came to a jarring stop,
and reached for the binoculars. A long-haired figure, male
or female, I couldn't be certain, seemed to be in trouble.
With "its" back toward me, this person appeared to be
clutching the rocks as "it" hung, feet downward, over raging whitewater at the lake's outlet. I pictured bare toes
wedged in cracks in the flat, clifflike rock as the person
struggled to climb back to safety. As I watched, the body
slumped forward as if exhausted. I could see no other
person around. God! I walked as fast as I dared, keeping
my eyes fixed on the terrain. When I finally arrived at
the outlet, the girl was sitting quietly on the rock, dangling bare feet as she looked down at the rushing water.
What in the hell had she been doing? Damn these strang-
ers in my wilderness! I forgot that I was thirsty; all that I
wanted to do was get on my way.

The lump was still in my throat as I headed down
toward Lace Lake. Suddenly someone above me started
shooting with a powerful gun. Bang, bang, bang. Some
people just can't stand the silence of wilderness. Damn
people with guns in this paradise! In the small camping
area at the inlet of Lace Lake are three small, flat spaces
where one can lay a bedroll or pitch a small tent. Two of
these spaces were covered with fresh horse shit, the third

was littered with wrappings and cans. Damn people with horses in this fragile alpine country! I picked up the litter, climbed out of the basin, then headed down the mountain toward the trailhead. Long before I reached the car park I had regained my sense of humor and was again at peace with the weekend tourists. In the parking area I found an ancient vehicle. On its rusted bumper was bolted the following message: "Yes, I'll give up my gun—when someone pries my cold dead fingers from around it." I didn't need to wonder where the folks who had arrived in that vehicle were camped.

A day in early June 1976 was chock-full of contrasts, even by mountain standards. When I turned the horses into the lower meadow that morning, the entire eastern sky was a sea of brilliant color. A short time later we were blessed with a gentle rain. At noon I sat eating in the pleasant sunshine on a high ridge in the Missions. When I had finished eating, I noticed something strange happening in the west. Dense, white, almost luminous clouds were rising about MacDonald Peak west of the divide, nuzzling Panoramic Peak as they boiled over the divide, then turning north and following the eastern face as far as my eyes could follow. Although these unusual clouds were worrisome, I was fascinated by the sight.

Since I had a long way to travel, I started moving down the ridge, followed by the dogs. By the time we reached the trail the day was overcast. As we started to drive down the mountain, it poured. The skies dried, and dusk came early that night.

The Landscape

I crawled off to bed last night without making an entry in the journal simply because I was too damned tired to do so. Usually I travel alone with the dogs, but yesterday my friend Cal, the wilderness ranger, joined us. We had gained four thousand feet in elevation, two-thirds of it by trail, when we stopped for lunch on Panoramic Peak in the Missions. It was a bright day, and warm. In the "Montana blue" sky were lazy white clouds of interesting shapes. As we sat eating and looking out over the valley at the Swan Range, a golden eagle soared above us, then drifted south and out of sight When our legs were rested we dropped to Lake-of-the-Clouds, a lake I've looked down on from many high places, but had never visited. It is a pretty lake, somehow larger than I expected it to be, nestled in its high cirque on the Mission divide. As I looked about I tried to interpret my emotions. I had a feeling of accomplishment, to be sure, and the awe that beauty in nature will inspire. I also felt some nervousness, both because our next drop would be a steep one and because we had a long way to go before nightfall. Mostly, though, there was just an overpowering feeling of happiness, the joy of being alive.

We rock-hopped across the outlet, which at this time of year carries only a small amount of water, then climbed out of the cirque and looked down on Iceflow Lake, high in the basin of the south fork of Post Creek. The drop to Iceflow was steep but in no way alarming. We were not surprised to find only one small chunk of floating ice on its surface at this time of year.

While our walk down Post Creek lacked the loud roaring of the creek and the profusion of alpine flowers we had enjoyed on a trip through the drainage in late July a few years ago, this drainage is lovely at any time. Yesterday the creek carried no threat as it rushed over rocks and under snow-bridges. Water cascading down the mountainside from snowfields on MacDonald Peak seemed less eager to mate with the creek; its voice was a soft chortle rather than a boisterous laugh of springtime. At Cliff Lake we crossed the outlet and began our last steep climb of the day. My legs were starting to complain a bit, and perhaps the spirit was a little less willing as we made the climb to the saddle.

It was dusk by the time we'd covered the miles of trail from the saddle to the waiting Jeep. My legs had stiffened on the drive down the mountain; just climbing out of the vehicle was a chore. As I hobbled to the gate to turn the horses into the lower meadow to feed, the dogs in a last burst of enthusiasm clipped me from behind as they raced about the meadow. For a moment I lay quietly, then gingerly started moving arms and legs. Slowly I got to my feet and opened the gate. I don't know why, but as I walked toward the cabin all stiffness was gone. Nothing remained but fatigue and a feeling of thankfulness that I have life, the mountains, and the will to enjoy both.

I picture the bright fall day when we left the trail and started to climb, for no reason other than to see bright fall colors on the mountain above us. It was an easy climb in the less rugged northern end of the Missions. Views from the summit were pleasing, but a long, narrow, crescent-shaped series of high meadows which lay immediately below the Mission Divide as I looked toward the north held the greatest allure. It would be fun exploring those meadows as we walked back to the saddle and the trail. While I had no way of knowing if we could drop in safety down that side of the mountain, neither did I know that such a drop couldn't be made. I decided to risk it. If we were to find ourselves "cliffed up" on the descent, we would simply have to climb back to the summit. Without further thought I started down.

For me the spirit of adventure seems greatest when uncertainty adds slight tension to the challenge of wilderness. Our drop was a steep one, but I had bear grass, brush, and small trees to cling to for support, and the dogs had no trouble following. We did find cliffs, but there was always a safe passage between them. At no time did we drop any place where we couldn't have climbed back up. Finally we moved out onto the valley floor, skirted a small, rocky lake, and went on our way. Travel along this series of high meadows was great fun. The flowers were long gone, but we had the pleasing fall colors on the slopes. I saw no people sign, no fire circles or litter. We topped out above the small unnamed lake, high in the Cedar Lake basin, that I know so well and love so much.

We had just started our drop toward this lovely lake when I saw by the actions of Misty and Charlie, a short distance ahead, that something new and exciting had been added to our day. Going a few steps farther, I saw the rear end of a mountain goat as it tried desperately to put distance between us. Since we had approached from above, its surprise was complete. Rarely have I moved so fast and accomplished so little. With my eyes on the goat and talking softly to the dogs, I struggled wildly to get the pack off my back. Still keeping my eyes on the climbing animal I pawed through the day pack, feeling for the camera. It was almost with relief that I saw the goat disappear among a cluster of large boulders above us. From the shore of my little lake I watched the goat make its final climb to the crest of the divide, then disappear from view. A mountain goat, fall colors, a bright day, this lovely little lake—who could ask for more? A drink of water, a few hastily snapped pictures, and we were off on the high contour which would take us back to the saddle and the trail of the morning. I don't know what the dogs were thinking, but I was savoring each event of the day.

August 7, 1978

A soul-satisfying day in the Missions. The country was fresh, the bear grass blooming in profusion. We climbed leisurely. I studied tiny flowers, located pockets of snow which I balled and ate for moisture, sought and examined unusual rock formations. The views from Point St. Charles were exceptionally clear; there was almost a complete absence of haze. I stood for a time looking at my old friends, those peaks and lakes that I've seen time after time, yet which always have something new and fresh about them. Those rugged peaks to the south appeared unusually clear today, and for the first time I was able to see Summit Lake at the base of Mount Harding in the north. Below me, to the west, lay Lake-of-the-Clouds, still frozen except for a narrow strip of open water at its edge. I saw no camper at any of the lakes below me; a good feeling for one who likes to travel alone.

It is never easy for me to leave a place of such beauty. On the drop back down the mountain I happened upon a small mountain meadow complete with tiny streams and miniature lakes, all formed by melting snow. The area was filled with profusely blooming alpine flowers. A little lower on the mountain Misty alerted me to a whiskered hiker walking slowly below us. He had not seen us and since I knew that he would be no more eager to talk with us than we were to visit with him, we changed our line of travel. As we walked down the slabs high above Glacier Lake I saw a bird rise from the ground, hover in the air, then fly to a low snag where it perched as though it were eager to be seen. It had seemed large when its wings were spread, but it appeared sleek and trim on its perch. A Townsend's solitaire. For the first time I was able to see the pale, rusty wing patch as described in bird guides.

Back at the trailhead, I glanced down and saw a folded bill lying on the ground. Twenty bucks is quite a sum to lose. I looked around at the parked cars. Had some person arriving in one of those cars, off God-knows-where in the hills, lost the money? Or had it been dropped by someone who left the parking area during the day? How could I hope to find the owner? Perhaps I grinned, for twenty bucks is also quite a sum to find! With a clear conscience I placed the money in my almost empty billfold, then drove on down the mountain.

July 26, 1979

I found alpine flowers blooming in profusion high above Island Lake in Mission country. Extensive flower fields lay along the base of craggy cliffs. High on the face of these cliffs soil has formed. In those high places were "window boxes" of multicolored blooms. The light just right for the proper display of such beauty. We climbed along beds of Indian paintbrush (salmon, flame, and deep scarlet in color). Whizzing from flower to flower was a female rufous hummingbird. After finishing her explorations she shot up to the flowers on the face of the cliff, then over the top and was gone. Higher on the trail were extensive beds of vetch mixed with penstemon and large, white flowers of bear grass. In smaller isolated areas I found forget-me-nots, yellow columbine, Townsendia, and alpine buttercups.

Finally I decided to try for the Mission divide, an off-trail climb I'd never made from this approach. We lunched on the crest, looking out over Post Creek in the Flathead Reservation, with Cliff, Disappointment, and First lakes, deep blue in color and very lovely, below us. Water poured over the cliff from Lake-of-the-Clouds and made its sheer drop to the valley floor below. I could see tiny Iceflow Lake high in the drainage. Snowmelt cascaded down MacDonald Peak. The roar of rushing water came up to me from both sides . While the dogs slept, I stayed on the crest, looking, listening and dreaming, for some time.

August 25, 1980

Today I introduced my friend Dave to my favorite little-known lake, high in the basin below the Mission divide. We left the trail at the saddle and started to climb. It was a pleasant day, cool and bright. We saw no people, nor did we hear people sounds. We stood on the highest point of the ridge, looking about, breathing the good air, thankful to be there. There was just enough haze to enhance the beauty of distant mountains. To the north we looked toward the stately mountains of Glacier National Park, and to the east we looked over the Swan Range at the mountains in the Bob Marshall wilderness. Below us in all directions we saw lakes of many sizes and shapes.

With a sigh of regret because we thought we should move on, yet with a feeling of pleasant anticipation, we dropped to my tiny lake below. As we walked to its shore, Dave spotted goats on the mountain above us. At first we saw only two adults, then a kid walked into view. The family moved slowly up the ridge and disappeared over its crest. We lunched while looking across the water at the steep slope of the Mission divide. Then we lounged for a time, resting and dreaming. When we had had our fill of idleness we started our high contour back to the saddle. We were both pleasantly weary as we drove down the mountain, mentally at great peace. Even the dogs seemed content to snooze, Charlie with her muzzle resting on my thigh, Misty snuggled up to Dave. What better way is there of cementing friendships and enjoying life?

Chapter Three

COMPANIONS

I arrived in this valley with two mares, one of them pregnant, and three dogs. To complicate our life in this new home, the dogs tangled with porcupine, chased deer, and treed bear. The horses, Nipper and Socks, caused less excitement. Then along came Piccolo, the new filly.

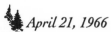 *April 21, 1966*

At four-thirty this morning I lay awake wondering if I should walk to the barn to see if my horse friend Socks had delivered during the night. Since I've made several early-morning trips down to the horses and have always found things as they were the night before, I decided to forget it, and instead picked up a book and started reading. But at five I relented. I climbed out of bed and glanced outside, then grabbed my pants and ran for the barn. The filly lay in a snow bank. The newborn is a doll, dark brown in color, a white star on her forehead. She has four white feet.

Three days later I noted that Socks had been meaner than sin since her filly was born. She would allow none of us to approach her child. Yet when I ride off on Nipper, Socks seems jealous. When we return from the ride she allows me to pet her briefly, then throws her ears back and threatens to bite. Ah, motherhood!

By the latter part of June, Piccolo, so named because of her frequent, high-pitched neighing, was beginning to acquire some gray hairs in her dark coat. She was a beautiful animal, the pride of both mother and aunt. I loved watching her as she led the old girls from meadow to barn at a canter. Then, late in July, the queens of my stable turned my peace into shambles.

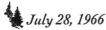 *July 28, 1966*

I was reading in bed tonight when sounds coming from the meadow indicated trouble. I found Piccolo, the young filly, running back and forth outside the meadow fence while mother and aunt charged about. When I opened the pole gate, trying to keep the opening just large enough for the filly to come through, Nipper charged out and joined Piccolo. Nice going, cowboy! Now only the mother was inside the fence. Using pellets as a bribe, I lured the filly back into the meadow. But snorty, feisty Nipper liked her freedom and would have none of me. I closed the gate and walked to the barn with both mother and daughter following me and the pellets. My strategy seemed to be working; Socks walked into her stall. Then, as I reached out to close the gate, she charged, striking my outstretched hand and knocking me to the floor. Without my being aware of it the filly had sauntered out of the barn and her mother wasn't about to be separated from her daughter again.

Filled with self-pity, knowing painfully that my wrist was broken, I lay on the floor. Just as I started to get up

I heard the twang of breaking barbed-wire. Gentle, reasonable, sweet-tempered Nipper, the girl who had refused to come in when the gate was open, had changed her mind. She had seen us walk into the barn; she wanted pellets, too. So she had run around to the west side of the meadow and charged through a temporary, two-strand barbed-wire fence. Now she stood trembling in the moonlight, bleeding from a long gash in her chest wall.

Over a period of months, Piccolo traded her dark coat for one of gray, but kept her black mane and tail. She was strikingly beautiful. Since I didn't want to destroy her trust in me, even briefly, I had postponed her weaning. Each day, however, it became more obvious to me that if this child was ever to be weaned, I would have to start the process.

 February 4, 1967

A few days ago I decided that Piccolo should be weaned. Under protest Socks has remained in the barn for the last three days. The filly now wears a halter with nails protruding from its nose strap. I have been told that a mare whose bag is swollen and sore will reject a greedy filly when her bag is pricked by these nails. Today I opened the barn door, let Socks into the meadow, and waited for the fun. Piccolo didn't go to her mother then, but a few hours later I saw her nursing, gingerly to be sure, but definitely nursing. Perhaps a smaller halter would help.

Piccolo was most gentle when I removed the halter, but she would have none of its replacement. She was mad, mad, mad! I tried to make the exchange in Pic's stall but she jumped over the manger and out two times before I finally gave up. Nursing now continues without a halter, much to the delight of both mother and child.

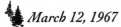 *March 12, 1967*

Since the failure of my first attempt at weaning the filly I've offered her nothing but love and kindness, hoping the little devil would forget past differences. This afternoon I decided to start over again. I theorized that it would be easier to replace the halter if I placed a noose around her neck first. The idea may have been sound, but its execution was faulty. In my nervousness the loop I placed about her neck was much too large. Before I could tighten it she had put a foot through it. Removing the rope then proved to be more difficult than the original application had been. This little girl hadn't forgotten any part of our previous struggle and she had no thought of cooperating with me today. Before we left that stall Piccolo wore her halter. She had a superficial cut on one front leg which resulted, I suppose, when she ran against the boards dividing the two stalls. I was pooped but uninjured.

When the time came for training, Piccolo went off to school. I had trained her mother myself, but wanted this girl to be professionally trained. From time to time I visited one of her training sessions. It gave me pleasure to see her progress and to note the mutual respect between horse and trainer. Piccolo now gives a fine ride, but she must never be taken for granted.

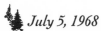 *July 5, 1968*

Not all rides begin smoothly. When we were starting off this morning I noticed that the door into the basement was open. I climbed down, dropped the reins, walked to the cabin and closed the door. As I started back toward the patient horse I saw her mother charg-

ing around the corner of the barn. I had shut Socks in
her stall thinking to avoid trouble, but there she was,
trouble. Before I could reach the saddled horse, she began running wildly outside the fence, dragging her reins,
as she responded to her mother's antics. I had no chance
of catching either horse without a bribe, so I ran to the
barn for pellets. I caught Socks and led her toward the
barn. Piccolo had seen the pellet can, too. I glanced back
just as the saddled mare tried to jump the pole gate. She
landed on the upper pole and straddled it, kicking with
all four feet as she tried to propel herself forward. Finally
the pole cracked, allowing the excited horse to reach the
ground. She ran toward the barn for pellets, still dragging her reins.

Even though the horses have just been boarders for the
past few years, they still have moments when they assert their
right to a place on center stage. I'd finished the new pole
fence near the cabin, had hauled a tank of water from the
creek for the stock tank, and was raking a snow-free bit of
lawn when Piccolo decided to roll. The idea was not a bad
one; what made this roll different from hundreds of others
she had taken was that she started her roll too close to the
meadow fence. When I first saw what she was up to she was
lying on her side *under* the lower rail. I ran toward her, although I had no idea what I planned to do when I reached
her. As I started my run the mare suddenly realized that she
was in trouble and panicked. With a mighty heave she got to
her feet, the fence still on her back. Much to my surprise,
when the horse charged out from under the fence, it snapped
back into place without collapsing.

But Piccolo was now outside the fence, her mother still in the meadow. Neither horse liked the world as she saw it. I opened the gate, hoping that Pic would join her mother, then looked behind me to see Socks charging toward the opening on her way out. I shouted, swore, waved my arms. Socks managed to swerve as I closed the gate. I walked to the barn for a halter and pellets, but when I tried to bribe Piccolo with pellets she would have none of them or me. Obviously she regarded me as the cause of her entrapment. She also was having a great time running back and forth with Frosty barking up a storm behind her. Socks, too, refused pellets.

In disgust I stomped back to the barn, rattling the pellets in the can, hoping that this white horse that loves to eat would follow me. I poured pellets into her feed box, then ignored the old girl as I walked back to the cabin. When Socks realized that she could eat pellets without being shut up in her stall she walked into the barn. Now that her mother was in the barn and her friend Frosty was no longer interested in the chase, Piccolo found freedom to be less exciting. When I opened the gate she charged back into the meadow. She was uninjured except for a bloody nose and a badly hurt pride. I closed the gate and walked away. I thought, to hell with both of them!

The dogs have caused similar joys and troubles, as already mentioned. Old Pooh, the oldest and a Norwegian elkhound, was the least active. For the most part, she lay about sleeping. Then she died a natural death. Waif, a golden retriever, was sweet-natured and people-oriented as most goldens are. My feeling for her is adequately expressed, I think, in a note written late in January of 1969.

—We did a lot of walking today, traveling on the road since poor old Waif, who loves to come with us, can't travel well in deep snow. This old dog still makes time. She forges ahead, then waits for me with tail wagging and a loving smile on her face. She's ill, though, and I doubt that she will be walking with us much longer.

Penny, my elkhound pup, was just a few weeks old when I arrived here, and developed into a fine companion. Then one afternoon late in October of 1971, my seven-year-old friend met a hunter with a gun.

November 1, 1971

Although my heart wasn't in it I drove across the mountain today for my new Samoyed pup. When I first saw the litter—seven five-week-old, white, powder puffs with black noses and eyes—the pups were standing on their hind legs in a large carton, their forefeet up on the carton wall, clambering for attention. I wanted a female; there were six in the litter. How could I possibly choose? As I watched, one pup dropped to the floor of the carton, grabbed the tail of the pup next to her, and pulled like mad. I grabbed the pup, found it was female, and closed the deal. With that personality, I thought, she should do well in my peculiar household.

November 6, 1971

Slowly the pup is finding her own place in this strange household. I think it will be a place of great importance. Yesterday she developed a diarrhea. Although I put her outside three times during the night, I still stepped barefoot in puppy poop this morning. As I was cleaning this up the little devil squatted and started to pee. That did it! With a whoop I pounced, cuffed her, and tossed her outside.

Today when I was burning downfall in the timber, Misty was underfoot much of the time. She tugged on branches I was dragging to the fire; I was afraid that she would be stepped on or burned. Later, when I shed my jacket and laid it at the base of a tree, my tired friend climbed on it and went to sleep. Why hadn't it occurred to me that perhaps she didn't wish to be underfoot, that she may just have been afraid of being lost? My jacket is now her security blanket.

That winter when the snow was fresh I sometimes lost my white friend. It was always easier to find her when the sun was shining, since the little dog cast a large black shadow. Late in March, when deer returned to the block across the pond, I found Misty with forefeet up on a log, watching them with great interest. The Samoyed had an insatiable curiosity. Her first real confrontation with deer came later. She had come to the barn with me and lay out in the meadow, drowsing, while I worked in the loft. I watched as a doe and her yearling fawn walked slowly toward the dog. As Misty paid no attention to the deer, the larger animal stomped the ground with a front foot, then blew loudly. Startled by the sound of the blowing the dog got to her feet. She watched as both deer slowly high-stepped from the meadow.

My dogs had all been females, none of them spayed. We had had no problems here in the hills because of our isolation. Then one day when Misty was in heat, a small, black male entered our lives.

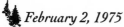 *February 2, 1975*

For more than nine years I've been casual, almost to the point of carelessness, about my females in heat, simply because we live so far from amorous males. But a small, black-spotted lover has found us. I suppose we walked too far toward the highway on our hike yesterday and the little bastard found the notes Misty left by the roadside. The moment I open the cabin door, pellet gun in hand, the dog is out of sight, hidden by the high banks of snow along the shoveled walk. Although most of this day has been filled with irritations, my luck turned toward evening. I'm still laughing. The little guy ran as usual, but this time I jumped in the pickup and followed. Snow banks at the roadside were almost too high for him to climb, and if he did reach their crest he couldn't travel in the soft, deep snow beyond. I ran him for three miles at twenty miles an hour, slowing only toward the last when he seemed to falter. He may be back tomorrow, but his expression as he left implied he'd not be with us tonight.

That little spotted dog, so filled with lust and determination, caused us no harm. However, in October of the same year when Misty was again in a receptive mood, a dog belonging to an outfitter traveling through my property was more successful. I'd taken my eyes off my friend for only a moment to watch a rainbow over the Swan Mountains. When I looked back she was gone.

December 9, 1975

A crisis in the family! The actions of my white friend worry me. If she took the packer's dog in October, and I think she did, she should deliver about December 14. I've watched her closely and have maintained until this morning that she is not pregnant. Today she has been acting strangely and didn't come to my whistle. I found her in her doghouse, a place she uses only under protest. She stayed there all morning, even though the kennel gate was open. Perhaps I crawled in the house to check her too many times this morning; at any rate, she disappeared again this afternoon. When she did come to my whistle, her belly and legs were covered with mud. By following her tracks I found that she had crawled into an old badger den under some downfall. She watched me from the bunkhouse when I fed the horses, but when I finished in the barn she was gone again. I'm wondering if she is looking for a place to deliver where she can have some privacy. I've been out many times tonight looking for her by flashlight. Sometimes I wonder if the dog depends on me, or if I depend on her. Now, late in the evening, she's just come up the walk. I put her in her kennel and closed the gate. What a screwed up day this has been!

December 10, 1975

When I walked to the kennel early this morning I heard pups crying in the doghouse. Flashlight in hand I crawled into the house and found, if I wasn't hallucinating, pups in the bread line from stem to stern. Misty licked them continuously, tumbling them about so that a reliable count was not possible. I'd say that there were at least six, their colors ranging from black to brown, their markings from spots to stripes.

When the time came to part with the pups I naturally kept one, a little black-and-white female. Officially named Charlotte, she's always been called Charlie. In her quiet way Charlie has added her bit to the fun of living. One afternoon the dogs flushed a snowshoe rabbit. In its blind haste the rabbit collided with Charlie who was then about three months of age. The frightened pup tore up the hill to the cabin, howling all the way.

Charlie began her high-country hiking career at the age of six months. Initially, the pup hesitated in attempting a climb which to her looked difficult. At these times I indicated to Misty the route which I thought would be the easiest for Charlie. Misty then made the climb and stood waiting at the top for her daughter. When the pup joined her mother she was given an enthusiastic face-licking. When I reached them, Charlie was praised and petted. After a few days of this treatment the pup needed no more encouragement. Then, one day later in the summer, these roles were reversed. Both dogs made a short climb with ease, but because of the danger of slipping on wet, moss-covered rock, my own climb was made slowly and with care. As my head appeared at the top, while my hands were still clinging to supporting rocks, both dogs licked my face with enthusiasm.

Then came Charlie's first hunting season, during which she had a lesson on the evils of gluttony. We had had rain during the night and there was a temporary snow line on the wooded slopes behind the cabin. It seemed an ideal morning for burning brush piles. Occasionally during the morning I heard gunshots reminding me that the big push was on to put game in the freezer. Early in the afternoon I noticed Misty as she trotted off into the forest with her nose in the air. Just where the hell did she think she was going? Since the brush fires were low and the countryside wet, I followed with

Charlie walking beside me. Near the western border of the property both dogs gave me the slip, and neither came to my whistle. Still gun-shy from the senseless shooting of Penny I was worried and mad. With hunting season in full swing and two dogs on the loose, I suppose I had reason to be. Did I dare wander about looking for them wearing a faded denim jacket?

Scolding ravens across the fence interrupted my thoughts. Such noises usually meant the ravens were feeding on deer remains; my dogs were probably there, too. Forgetting I needed to wear some identifiably human color, I climbed through the fence and found both dogs feeding on bloody deer guts left by a successful hunter. Misty had heard the ravens from our work site and had gone to share in the bounty.

I brought the dogs home, fed them, and chucked them in the kennel while I cooked my own meal. Later in the evening when Charlie disappeared again I knew where to find her. She was there, but ran for home as soon as she saw me. Back at the cabin I found two piles of vomit on the walk; one pile of bloody meat and one pile of dog food. Relieved that her stomach was now empty, I thought no more about it. Then sometime during the night I heard Charlie retching in the living room, rushed to the door, and threw her out. When I turned on the light I found three small masses of bloody meat piled neatly on the rugs. I had forgotten that first meal stolen from the protesting ravens.

Misty was growing older but two veterinarians had said that age nine was not too old for breeding. This Samoyed had been such a fine companion that I wanted to try for another like her. So I introduced her to a lusty, registered Samoyed male. The encounter surprised my friend, but I sensed no resentment. Only one live pup resulted from this breeding; Misty went to surgery for the removal of a uterus near rupture because of one dead pup that she had not been able to expel. Frosty, a handsome male, plans to be a lady's man, just like his father.

Before Frosty was ten months of age he had tangled with a porcupine. He got another surprise early one fall when he leaped into a nest of wasps at the side of a high-country trail. I saw him leap, saw him fighting something with his mouth and paws, then watched as he rolled onto his back and fought with everything he had. Not until then did I see the wasps swarming about him. I ran back up the trail, calling the dogs as I ran. We were all stung, of course. Later, when the swarm seemed to have settled back into their nest, we skirted the area in the timber and went on our way. At the outlet of the lake Frosty lay in the cold water for some time with only his head above the surface. He must have had innumerable stings. On the five-mile jaunt back to our Jeep this young-ster stayed at my heels. He wasn't sure what had happened, but he made certain that he didn't ask for more.

Chapter Four

PREDATORS AND PEOPLE

In these hills are scores of predators, supposedly vicious killers put on this earth for the sole purpose of being trapped, shot, and poisoned. Anyone who professes to enjoy seeing these "varmints" must be odd indeed. Some folks overlook the fact that man is the greatest predator of all.

I have seen domesticated canines chasing deer on several occasions, but only once in twenty-one years have I seen a coyote running a deer. I realize now, although I didn't at the time, that the doe was old and not well. She was running heavily when she broke out of the timber and ran toward us with the coyote behind her. Neither animal seemed to notice us until Penny, the elkhound, charged her hated coyote enemy. The coyote turned back into the timber with my friend at its tail. The doe ran free.

On my arrival in the valley, old timers warned me that the coyote, a killer by instinct, would lure my dogs into the brush and kill them. For this reason I was uneasy when I knew that coyotes were about. I recall my nervousness on one of my early rides, when I saw the head of a coyote peering from behind a boulder. Penny either ignored the coyote or didn't see it. Next, the coyote watched us from behind a low clump of brush, much too close; the dog charged into the brush after it. The sounds which I heard then could mean only hard fighting — or so I believed until my friend returned to me looking much too smug and pleased with herself to have been involved in anything but a battle of words. The coyote trailed us at a discreet distance for the rest of the ride.

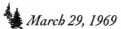

March 29, 1969

As we walked up the logging road toward the cabin Penny seemed nervous and preoccupied. On two occasions she had run ahead, then ignored me when I whistled. She refused to come to me so that I could put her on the leash. This was unlike her. A little farther up the road she trotted over a ridge and started to bark. Only then did I hear the coyotes. When Waif and I reached the top Penny trotted to us. The two coyotes showed no concern when we suddenly appeared, but neither did they leave. Both were beautiful. The female, the smaller of the two, sat across the shallow ravine watching us with interest. The larger male sat much closer. Both had coats of long, golden-brown hair with an overlying silver cast. From time to time the male pointed his muzzle toward the sky, then broke into song. As I watched through the glasses he seemed very close indeed. The pair stayed for some time, then trotted leisurely into the timber.

For many months, that year, coyotes seemed to haunt my place. Early one October morning I heard a coyote yipping across the fence. Penny barked her reply, and deer left the meadow. When I fed the horses I found the dog barking again near the meadow fence. With each foray into the property beyond the fence she drove a coyote back, but when she turned, the coyote followed her back to the property line. At times I heard sounds of fierce fighting but I suspect there was no actual body contact between the two. Both horses, interested onlookers, stood watching the charade.

Somehow this dog of mine seemed to know which coyotes she cared to discipline, and which she had better leave alone.

 *February 18, 1971*

When Penny left the cabin this morning she gave me the impression that she had matters of great importance on her mind. Later, as I threw hay to the horses, I heard her barking across the fence to the west. I found my friend holding two beautiful coyotes at bay. The animals were large, each larger than the elkhound. When I appeared they trotted off a few feet, then sat quietly watching me. It was obvious that they knew me and that they could have harmed the dog had they wished to do so. Can this be a game?

As I wandered through the timber on snowshoes one morning coyotes suddenly burst into song ahead of me. The elkhound listened for a moment, then trotted off among the trees. A short time later I heard her barking. I continued my climb, stopping now and then to look and to listen. I happened to be standing quietly when a large, good-looking coyote trotted out of the brush, leaped up on a snow-covered log, and looked back in the direction from which it had come. Perhaps this boy hadn't seen me as he didn't look my way, but it seemed evident that he knew that the elkhound was tracking him. He jumped from the log and went on his way only moments before Penny trotted out.

On many occasions I have seen a coyote's potential prey show a studied indifference to the presence of the predator. Late in May one year, two deer stood at the mineral block down meadow casually watching a coyote across the water. They continued watching as the coyote worked its way around the end of the pond. Not until the animal was quite close to them did they send their white-tipped tails up and high-step from the meadow. The coyote showed no interest in the deer. It only stopped for a moment to sniff around the block before it trotted off on the same trail.

 *May 22, 1968*

 This was a dull, wet morning made more pleasant by the sight of both deer and elk feeding in the lower meadow. Four geese flew in, landed on the pond, then walked out on the grass to feed. Some time later when the deer and elk were gone, a coyote trotted across the meadow. Although the predator was not more than a dozen feet from the geese when it passed them, the geese took no more than a casual interest in the coyote.

On another spring day an attractive and pregnant coyote stood near the shore of the pond, looking toward the cabin. A mallard pair that had been swimming about in the center of the pond sat on the water looking up at the coyote. The predator ignored the ducks.

Coyotes are usually silent, but they can be vocal when the mood is right. The infrequently heard but long-continued yipping of a coyote sets my teeth on edge; I give thanks that I'm not a deer. But I shall never tire of coyote song. In the early 1970s when the coyote numbers were greater, we heard more singing. The low price placed upon their fur in those years made their destruction financially less rewarding. I find a different reward in their live choruses.

December 9, 1973

The temperature this morning was ten above zero, the day clear and bright, the afternoon warm. When I walked back to the fire tonight the moon was full, the night still. I stood looking at the flames, absorbing the warmth of the fire, breathing the crisp, good air, and enjoying the evening. A coyote called softly several times. I never cease to be amazed at the variations in the songs these animals sing. They sing for their own enjoyment, I'm sure. At times, like the human who hums, the coyote seems to ad-lib, adding notes or soft barks where they seem to fit. The song tonight was fleetingly lovely, the setting ideal.

October 7, 1969

At dusk Penny and I left the cabin to throw more wood on our fires. There were no disturbing sounds. I'd been working for some time when the stillness was broken by the singing of a coyote in the east. This song was answered by two coyotes in the south, then by an animal in the west. For a time we seemed surrounded by coyotes, none of them far from my work site. I stood listening for a long time, then looked about for Penny. She was sitting near me. She, too, had been listening.

The night was a dark one. When we walked out of the cabin the only sounds to be heard were the organlike calls in the west. The calls, repeated over and over, were essentially the same. When the soloist finally finished I heard what sounded like a crowd of cheering people. The cheering sections were coyotes, of course, as was the soloist.

 *November 6, 1972*

When I stepped out of the cabin tonight a coyote sang across the pond. The song was soft and so lovely that I stood listening until the singer moved on. Later, all hell broke loose in the lower meadow. Many coyotes broke into song, each animal trying to out-sing the others. Added to the bedlam was the off-key singing of Misty. I walked to the meadow fence but could see nothing in the darkness. I whistled for the dog. Each of my whistles caused a diminished volume of coyote song, just as each turn of a dimmer switch will decrease the intensity of light. Not until the last coyote had ended its song did my young friend trot out of the darkness and come to me.

Misty, the Samoyed, has never developed the elkhound's intense hatred of coyotes. One October evening as I worked outside the cabin, coyote songs came at me from many directions. At dusk the singing started again, this time all coyotes in the timber on the east side of the lower meadow. I left the cabin, both to listen to the song and to see what, if any, effect this song had on Misty. At first, because of the darkness I could see nothing. Then I found the white figure dashing about the meadow, as if in play. Not until the play brought the animals closer to me was I able to make out the indistinct figure of the coyote she was playing with.

I also have this white dog to thank for a unique serenade one Christmas morning. Although Misty was coming in heat she harbored no resentment toward a large, sexy coyote male when he checked the property several times daily. Shortly after daylight on Christmas morning I saw this coyote circle the rear of the cabin, then take his stand on the hill a short distance from the cabin window. There he stood watching two coyotes at play in the meadow, squatted to urinate, and resumed his watch. The coyotes in the meadow started to sing. For a time the big male stood watching, but it seemed that the urge to join in was overpowering. He threw back his head, opened his mouth, and burst into song. The coyotes in the meadow gradually stopped their serenade and stood watching the soloist on the hill.

One day in August we were piped down the mountain at Red Butte by a coyote. We had had a good climb, enjoyed old scenes, and were on our way down the mountain by a new route. I had been struggling over downfall, pushing my way through brush, and trying to avoid boulders on my way to the cutting unit below us. The dogs were leading when a coyote started its calling ahead of us. Both dogs trotted back to me. As we moved down the mountain the coyote moved ahead of us. I judged by the sound of its calls that it was keeping the distance between us constant. Then, for a short time, there was silence. When we next heard the animal call, it was behind us. We were followed by the animal until we reached the cutting unit; then there were no more calls.

Perhaps a charge of predation can be lodged against any meat-eater unless the animal or bird eats only carrion. These accusations are usually spoken softly unless the prey is something owned or desired by man. Although badgers are said to eat anything in the meat or egg line, whether freshly killed or carrion, complaints against them relate chiefly to their digging habits. A foraging badger digs large holes in which a horse may step and break a leg. One afternoon late in July Penny left Waif and me at the edge of the meadow, ran into the timber, then started barking in great excitement. She had cornered an animal in the brush, an animal whose hissing I could hear long before I was able to see it. The animal's stocky body was light brown, its legs were short and bowed, its tail short. The head of this less-than-friendly beast was flattened and a light, yellowish-tan streak extended across it, nose to neck. Similar streaks left each angle of the mouth and ran below the eye to the ear. The badger's ears were short and rounded and its teeth, prominently displayed by snarling lips, were sharp. On the defensive, Penny's new acquaintance crouched low and made digging movements with both front and rear feet as it moved slowly backward. None of us doubted that this little beast was ready for a fight. Whenever Penny moved too close the badger lunged at her. Finally I had seen enough, called the dogs, and we moved on.

Other predators in the Swan country have little effect on humans but deadly impact on wild things. The marten is said to be the red squirrel's public enemy number one. Although a marten will slaughter no more than it will eat, its presence means certain death to a long list of creatures. The marten I watched in the Missions one day seemed a picture of innocence. The dogs and I were on our way back to the vehicle when Misty stopped to visit with a friend she had just discovered sitting on a branch above the trail. Gruffly I told the dog to make tracks, that she could see squirrels back at the cabin. Then I looked up. I reached for the glasses and studied the animal; it was no squirrel. This animal appeared to be three times the size of our red squirrels. Its ears were large, its head small and the neck, as it was being extended, seemed endless. The throat and the breast of this beast were an attractive shade of yellowish-buff; the rest of the body and the head were a rich yellowish brown. Coarser guard hairs in its body fur were either dark brown or black in color. A bushy tail completed the picture. I think it was the large, questioning eyes that gave the animal its look of innocence. The marten gave no sign that it had seen us.

Of all the predators of meadow mice, the smaller weasels are said to be the most fearsome. They are described as rapacious hunters, frequently killing more mice than they can eat. On two interesting occasions I've encountered the least weasel, smallest of the weasel family. Late in September 1969, when I was cleaning up areas of logging slash and downfall, I wandered into a cutover area where I had not as yet done any cleaning. As I stood looking about me, wondering where I might pile and burn with minimum damage to new trees, I developed a feeling of restlessness, a feeling that I was being watched. I looked around me, but could see no one. When I glanced down I found a small, brown weasel with a white abdomen and toes staring intently up at me. Its curiosity satisfied, it scampered back into the piles of branches which I assumed it called home.

August 24, 1979

When the weather cleared about six this evening I climbed to the loft of the old barn and sat in the doorway, reading. A quick movement at my side caught my eye. At first I saw nothing, but as I watched a head appeared in the space between the makeshift floor and the door casing, then quickly disappeared again. The little creature seemed both spooky and curious. It reappeared several times, each time about a foot from my leg. Its small, flattened head was covered with fur in an attractive shade of brown. Its eyes were black and beady below small and rounded ears. Its chin, anterior neck, and the chest were yellowish-white. Since I didn't move, my curious friend became more confident. With its front paws up on the door sill, the little animal stretched its neck and body until I wondered where all this length could be coming from. At last my visitor gracefully climbed up on the door sill where it stood quietly for a time facing me. Then, with short, ladylike steps it moved slowly toward me. It was only an inch from my thigh when I flicked the corner of my paper. My friend was gone in a flash. I loved this encounter, but decided that an inch was close enough. The least weasel, it is said, can inflict a nasty bite.

Snakes are famed predators. My friends, the Berners, tell of a garter snake's predation on small fish in their pond. Water from Rumble Creek flows through a section of four-inch pipe then drops about a foot into the pond. Over a period of weeks the couple noticed a decline in the numbers of small fish in the water. They had also seen fish leap from the pond into the stream pouring from the pipe, much as salmon propel themselves through rapids. One day as they sat watching the water they noticed a garter snake poised above the pipe, a position the snake maintained until a small fish leaped from the pond into the stream of water. The snake struck, and missed. Again it coiled its body above the pipe. Another fish leaped into the stream; this time the snake didn't miss. The fish dropped back into the water pulling the snake into the pond with it. After a brief struggle the snake surfaced, alone. The fish had been too large for it to handle.

I, too, have seen snakes in action.

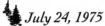 *July 24, 1975*

The trail along Piper Creek is long and steep in places. We were walking through a brushy portion of the trail when I noticed a large garter snake slithering diagonally across the trail toward me. Overhanging brush hid the snake's head, but I was able to see that while its movements were normal in rhythm, they were slow and labored. Just as the snake slithered into the brush I had a glimpse of what should have been the head. This snake was a deformed monster! Quickly I realized that what I had seen was a snake whose head had been hidden by the small, brown bird it was dragging. As I parted the brush at the side of the trail hoping for a second look, Misty high-stepped into the brush near me. Suddenly I heard the bird's wings beating on brush as it shot up into the air and was gone. The dog must have stepped on or near the snake and caused it to open its mouth. The bird was very much alive.

Some time later as we walked along the shore of Piper Lake, we met a dejected teenager who complained bitterly to me about the length of the trail and its steepness. His group had hiked to the lake the night before, carrying little on their backs because tents and food had been brought in by pack stock. Thinking that I might give him something to think about other than his own fatigue I told him about the snake with the bird. The unhappy chap looked at me, thought for a brief moment, then said, "I ain't never seen a snake eat." With these words spoken he quickly returned to his brooding.

About one year later I had a similar experience. I heard a rustle in the brush beside me. When I looked to see what had caused it I saw only a garter snake. But why hadn't this snake slithered away as they usually do? I stood quietly. The snake opened its mouth, then closed it on feathers. When the snake started to pull I saw that the feathers were part of a brown bird that was caught in the brush. The color of the feathers so closely matched the woody parts of the brush in which the bird was trapped that I had not seen it. The snake was tugging hard, yet could not dislodge it. When I moved closer the snake released its hold and disappeared down a hole nearby. Gently I removed the bird from the brush. It was a young bird, fully feathered. A small, superficial wound showed red on one wing, but the wing was not broken. A concerned, chirping sparrow perched in the tree above me. Since I could find no nest in the immediate vicinity, I decided that the young bird must have tried its wings, sailed into the brush, and been trapped there. With a nod to the parent I placed the young bird on a large stump, then walked on to check the ducks on a pond nearby.

On my return I found the bird still on its stump, but both bird and stump were now in full sunlight. The bird's mouth was open and it was panting. I shielded the overheated young one with a large piece of bark, then stood back to watch. Slowly its breathing became less rapid, its mouth closed, and it seemed to be resting. I could still hear the agitated parent in the vicinity. About eight that night I returned to the area. The youngster was not on its stump, nor could I find it anywhere on the ground. I like to believe that it may have flown off with its parent.

Snakes can also be enthusiastic lovers, it seems. I watched, one evening, as two seemed to be enjoying a few tender moments. At one of the ancient sawmill sites on the place I seemed to have broken up a gathering of garter snakes. My appearance sent snakes slithering away in all directions. It was obvious to me that something of importance was afoot. On my walk back to the cabin, that night, I passed a second sawmill site. Here on the slabs and sawdust I found seven snakes intertwined into a rough ball. I felt certain that this strange behavior must, in some way, be associated with reproduction. But how? Four years later I found my answer in the *National Geographic* magazine. In an article titled "Manitoba's Fantastic Snake Pits" published in the issue of November 1975, Michael Aleshiuk wrote that sometimes as many as a hundred males attempted to mate with one female at the same time. This produced huge mating balls in which the female couldn't be seen.

About mid-morning one bright day in February several years ago I finished my work in the cabin, then brought my clothes to the window so that I might dress while watching birds in the feeding area. My first glance told me that something was very wrong out there. Steller's jays flew about in great excitement. There were no small birds in sight. Beneath one of the feeders was what appeared to be a mass of brown feathers. Certain that a predator had made a kill, I opened the door and rushed outside for a better look. I suddenly became aware of the total picture. The predator, a boreal owl, sat on the ground clutching its kill, a gray jay; a nude male holding binoculars stood barefoot in the snow nearby. The temperature was ten degrees below zero.

Another time, as I walked toward the cabin door one noon, I heard the continuous flapping of large wings. It took but a moment to find the source of the disturbance. The mischievous pine squirrel that had been robbing my bird feeders much of the winter was clinging to a branch in the top of a lodgepole pine. A hawk, clutching the squirrel with its talons, was trying to dislodge the terrified squirrel with its powerful wings. Very slowly the squirrel relaxed its hold. When it had been pulled free the hawk dropped to the ground with its prey. Then with great effort the bird took off with the lifeless squirrel in its talons and glided into the forest.

There are times when predation is both fascinating to watch and beautiful to see. On a bright, comfortably warm day in late summer I and two friends relaxed on a bank above Glacier Sloughs in the Missions. A large bird appeared and flew over in wide circles. Suddenly it hovered on massive wings, then plummeted into the water. Its first dive was a clear miss, and a second was without success. But with its third dive the osprey flew away carrying a fish in its talons. A beautiful sight, this big bird diving in an expanse of water broken only in a few places by grass or reeds, with mountain peaks as the background. After lunch that day the osprey returned for an encore. Again we saw the circling, the graceful hovering, the sudden dive. We watched as the big bird struggled to the surface, then flew slowly out over the trees with its fish and was gone.

Many years, starting in late October and peaking in the first or second week of November, bald eagles flew in from great distances to feed upon salmon that came up MacDonald Creek in Glacier Park, to spawn. In October of 1983 I stood on the bridge over the creek watching this activity for the first time. The water below me was filled with dead and dying salmon; they had spawned and their life cycle was completed. On days of peak feeding these eagles are said to number two to three hundred. We arrived early in the season; I counted only thirty-two eagles perched in trees or standing on the shore of the creek, but this was more eagles than I'd seen in one place before. It was obvious that these were not hungry birds. Occasionally an eagle dropped from its perch, grasped a fish, and started to fly off with the fish in its talons. Frequently, then, a second eagle would fly after the bird with the food, and steal the fish. Earlier gluttony seemed now to have been replaced by a game. Ducks and water ouzels went about their business in the creek without apparent fear of the predators in the trees above them.

The relationship between predator and prey is not always clear. From inside their cabin, my friends, the Berners, watched a large bobcat walk warily toward the body of a road-killed doe that the couple had dragged to the edge of their meadow. To their surprise, since it was mid-afternoon, the cat ate quietly in the open for about an hour. Suddenly they noted a subtle change in the bobcat's stance; its ears dropped, and its back arched. This was the cat's welcome for a wolverine that walked through the timber toward the carcass. When the wolverine saw the bobcat it slowly began to circle the bobcat on the carcass. Each slow circle brought the wolverine closer. This was an exciting time for the watchers, but just as the binocular-wielding couple thought a fight was inevitable, they heard a car racing up the mountain road, its horn blaring. The show was over! The wolverine disappeared into the timber in the direction from which it had come; the cat faded in among the trees. When the would-be ambulance driver drove into Dr. Berner's yard with his cargo, a patient with a cut finger, there was no sign that other visitors had so recently departed.

Cats are feared and seldom-seen predators.

September 30, 1971

Two times yesterday I found a thin, unattractive housecat in the bird feeding area. As neither the elkhound nor the master will tolerate a cat in this sanctuary, I tried to persuade it in a gentlemanly, rock-heaving way, to move on. Later, I was giving the horses their pellets when I heard Penny barking off in the brush. The dog was acting strangely; she traveled in circles, jumping over brush and downfall, barking hysterically. I picked up a rock and moved quietly toward her only to find that she had discovered two very small kittens. One was perched on a stump, its tail drooping and its body trembling. The other stood with its back arched, spitting mad. Damn! I called Penny and walked to the cabin hoping that a predator would take the kittens during the night.

This afternoon the dog went wild again. I was in the shower when I heard the dog barking, this time in the brush near the side of the old barn. I slipped on shorts and sneakers and dashed outside. Since the mother cat was up a tree I thought the dog had rediscovered the kittens. I ran toward the old building, whistling and calling. Penny trotted toward me — but the animal that leaped out of the brush and landed at my feet was no kitten. It looked up into my eyes, then was gone around the corner of the barn before I was fully aware of what had happened. It was followed by a hysterically barking dog. A whistling, pleading adult ran far in the rear. I had just seen my first mountain lion!

The mountain lion is a shy animal; few people ever see one. When I told my story to the group at dinner that evening, I learned that the mewing of the kittens that now lived among the woodpiles in the old barn had attracted a mountain lion that happened to be passing by. A female lion might wish to mother them; for a male they would make a good meal.

Not so rare as lions, bears are hated by many in the West. Twenty-seven years of life in this valley have given me no reason to dislike them. There are troublesome bears, of course, just as there are troublesome humans, but so frequently we create our bear problems by leaving garbage at the back door, nailing suet to a tree trunk for the birds, or simply lacking understanding and fearing things that are wild. It also is easier to profess hatred for an animal than it is to protest such hatred.

Although I feel reasonably certain that Piccolo, the mare, had never had an unpleasant encounter with bruin, she had an inborn dislike for the animals. I recall a morning ride in June during the early years of my stay here. The horse had been unusually docile until we left the trail and turned down an old, grass-grown skid road. When she saw two large bears ambling down the road ahead of us she stopped. Penny hadn't seen the bears, but Pic had and she had no intention of taking another step toward them. Only under protest did she stand while I glassed the twosome. We turned back toward the trail, and she danced all the way down the mountain.

Penny, the elkhound, took as much pleasure in chasing

bears as she did in sparring with coyotes. I had stepped outside, barefooted and in pajamas, early one June morning to view my mountain world. For a time I watched the hummers at the feeders and studied the peaks above me. Then yawning and stretching, I turned back toward the cabin. A half-completed yawn died suddenly when I saw a large brown bear sitting on its haunches behind a low bush not far from me. It was watching me with unfeigned interest. An involuntary gasp from me alerted the dog who lay asleep at the side of the cabin. She came on the run; the chase was on.

I recall a hellishly hot afternoon late in July when I chose to work at the typewriter in the cool cabin rather than brave the heat and work in the open. I happened to glance outside just as the head of a bear appeared above the brush in the feeding area. A few moments later the animal stepped into the open, ignoring the feeders and walking toward the cabin. It stood quietly about ten feet from the window. What a chance for a picture! I dove for the camera but just as I returned to the window the elkhound, who must have scented the bear, charged around the corner of the building ready for battle. The two were gone in an instant, the barking dog charging behind the running bear.

Other bear episodes are recounted in my journal.

August 12, 1969

I was reading in the cabin tonight with all windows open. Slowly I became aware of an unusual scratching noise which I thought originated at the south window. I listened, then heard it again. Quietly I walked to the window, leaned over a chair back, and looked down into the

eyes of a small black bear that sat with its forepaws on
the window screen. The scratching noise I'd heard had
been made by the slipping of claws on the screen. Although I enjoyed seeing the animal, I knew that any bear
at an open window was trouble. I shouted, but the bear
ran only a few feet, then turned to watch me. Penny had
been asleep on the floor in the bedroom. We walked out
of the cabin slowly— slowly, that is, until the dog picked
up the bear's scent. She must have treed the animal since
I heard her barking in the forest for a long time.

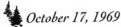 *October 17, 1969*

Penny woke me about midnight last night with a low
growl. Damn that dog! I thought. I ignored her first growl,
ignored the second, but crawled out of bed when she
growled a third time. She met me in the living room, telling me in every way she could that she wanted me to
open the door. I turned on the yard light, then opened the
door. Standing at the feeder tree, a short distance from
the cabin, stood a black bear, its front paws still clutching
the tree trunk. The doughnut feeder lay on the ground
below the tree. The position of the bear and its claw marks
on the bark told me that we had interrupted the animal as
it slid down the trunk after pulling the feeder from the
branch on which it hung. Neither bear nor dog were to
be seen a moment later, but I could follow their course by
the sounds of barking as they raced through the forest.

Misty, the Samoyed, who proved to be much more tolerant of coyotes than the elkhound, was also less disturbed by
bears. One evening early in the summer as we walked along
a grassed-in skid road, my white friend made a brief foray
into the timber. When she trotted back toward me she was

followed by a brown bear of medium size. Their pace, while brisk, was unhurried. While this picture in itself was most unusual, I soon learned that greater confusion was to follow. Misty knew that I was there, but when the bear looked up and saw me it turned quietly and ambled back into the timber. The dog couldn't have seen this action, but she obviously sensed the bear's change of direction, for she, too, turned and trotted back in among the trees. Misty came to me when I whistled but I saw no more of the bear. How does one explain such an unlikely tale?

About a year later when we were again tramping along an old logging road, we came up behind a black bear. We slowed our pace. The bear ambled slowly, occasionally stopping to snatch a mouthful of grass which it chewed and swallowed. I spoke softly to Misty who was several feet ahead of me. The bear must have heard my voice but I could see no reaction. Not until the dog turned back to join me did the bear bound into the timber as if pursued by devils.

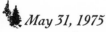 *May 31, 1975*

The morning was cool, bright and very lovely. Bird song seemed to come to me from all directions. Piccolo, the mare, was an angel at times, at other times acted the spirited bitch. An elk standing quietly in the brush below the road spooked her, but a short time later when we turned a switchback and found a bear walking up the road ahead of us she was calm. Although the bear must have heard the horse walking on the rocky road, it didn't look back or increase its pace. It walked slowly around a curve, then vanished. We stopped moving and I sat looking about. After a short wait the head of a black bear appeared above a large boulder at the side of the road. The animal's eyes never left us until we started moving again. Then with a sudden "swoosh" it was gone.

 *June 21, 1978*

Probably because of the overcast and its resulting decrease in visibility I've been less attentive to the great blue herons at their colony west of the Swan this year. Since it was bright and warm today I drove to the nest site, raised the binoculars casually, then snapped to attention. Standing over one of the nests was a black bear of medium size. It stood looking out over the valley, then turned and walked to the tree trunk where it disappeared from view. I marveled at its apparent unconcern about the limb on which it walked, since it was probably one hundred feet above ground. When I had last checked the nests there had been young birds in three of them and an adult bird sitting in each of the other two. Now I saw no life in any of the nests, nor were adult herons to be seen anywhere about the colony. The feeding of young herons is a noisy affair. The excitement and raucous calling begins when the adult bird appears and continues through the feeding. The tussle, when the eager young bird grabs hold of its parent's bill, looks like some sort of wrestling match. I suppose that the hungry bear had been attracted by the noise of a feeding and had climbed the tree to investigate.

It must have fed well. I saw neither adults, nor young, about the colony for the rest of the summer. The following year the nests had fallen into disrepair.

 July 1, 1985

I stopped suddenly and reached for the binoculars.

Across the pond, standing in the sunlight, was a large bear that sported a glossy, reddish-brown coat. With her were two cubs, probably about the size of a wet Samoyed. The cubs were light cinnamon in color. With my eyes fixed on the bears I started to move forward. When a tinder-dry branch broke beneath my foot with the sound of a gunshot, I froze. I needn't have; none of the animals looked my way. The sow was busily pulling apart downfall on the forest floor, then quickly lapping up the goodies exposed. Only rarely did she misjudge the state of rot in the fallen trunks. When she attacked a log that didn't give as she expected it to, she changed her approach. With a casual display of great power she fixed her long claws in a crack in the log, sat back on her haunches, and pulled. I heard scraping, then the sound of shattering log.

Neither cub seemed to be paying any attention to this activity. Perhaps they'd already had their lesson in "anting" and had other things on their minds. For a time both cubs rolled luxuriously in the long grass, then set about exploring the area. The most venturesome cub wandered out into the pond, walking on a log covered by water. It stopped, reached out a forepaw, and pulled something to the log. A noon snack of lily pad or pond weed, I suppose. I turned for a moment to check on the sow. When I focused on the cub again it was lying flat on its stomach on the water-covered log and was paddling furiously with all four legs. Practicing swimming, or just play time, I couldn't be certain. A short time later both swimmer and its sibling were again moving near their mother. With startling suddenness the sow raised to her haunches, forelegs in the air, and looked about in her nearsighted way. This was not the relaxed bear I had been watching. At the same moment two yellowish-brown bodies sailed through the air, each to a tree trunk. Both cubs quickly climbed to a height of about fifteen feet where they remained until the sow dropped to all four feet again. Then both youngsters slid back to the forest floor and resumed their explorations. Whether this had just been a training exercise for the cubs, I couldn't tell. Possibly the sow had scented me, or she may have heard some sound she questioned. This encounter gave me great pleasure. I wondered what would happen if I were to shout, then decided that I had no desire to see the bears run, either from me or toward me. Finally I backed slowly into the timber, walked back to the chain saw, then on to Frosty and the Jeep. Not until I arrived back at the vehicle did I realize that I had neglected to check the pond's surface for ducks, my reason for going to the pond in the first place.

One September Frosty, the young Samoyed, woke me to let me know that he had things to do which were better done outdoors. As he wandered off into the brush, I walked toward the outhouse. It was four-thirty in the morning. The moon was full, the countryside brilliantly lit, but the narrow, winding trail lay in shadow. I carried a lighted flashlight. I stepped up on the platform, heard the sudden scratching of claws on wood as an animal of some size scrambled to its feet, then felt the gentle shaking of the platform as the creature leaped to the ground below. The breathing of the running animal was strident, an odd mixture of grunt and wheeze, topped by a whistle. By the time I'd worked my way around a bench on the deck, and reached the edge of the platform, the animal was gone. Only the swaying of branches told me that it had passed that way. This was another first for me, a near encounter that must be credited to the bathroom needs of a young dog. I had disturbed a bear sleeping on the deck in the moonlight.

One midsummer evening in 1986 I had gone to the observation deck with a book. I had just stepped up on the platform when I saw a doe bounding across the grassy shore at the end of the pond. This lady was in one hell of a hurry! I was still watching when a large bear ambled out of the timber. With no hesitation it lumbered across the same strip of grassy shore, then disappeared among the trees in the direction taken by the panicked doe. I don't know what the intentions of the bear really were, but it doesn't take a brain to know what that deer thought its intentions were.

There are times when contact with these animals in the wild doesn't boost one's ego.

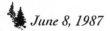 *June 8, 1987*

I stood swatting mosquitoes and trying to scan the surface of the pond for ducks. Then I heard Frosty bark, a bark which started as a boisterous challenge but which seemed to end in some doubt. Across a narrow strip of water near the pond's outlet I saw a cinnamon-colored bear. She looked mean! I could be certain of neither the dished face nor the hump of a grizzly, but on the four occasions when she raised to her hind legs to view us better, this bear was huge! Her two breasts were markedly enlarged; obviously she was nursing cubs. I studied her through the binoculars, but, since she seemed intent on remaining, I decided that we had best move on. I must admit some concern as we started to leave; walking slowly took control. Every time I turned for that "last look" I found her still glaring our way. When trees finally blocked my view I could only wonder if she was still there or if she was moving, and in which direction was she traveling? Frosty seemed to have forgotten her, but I was relieved when we finally reached the Jeep and climbed in.

*October 2, 1987*

At noon I noticed three unusual shapes on the nearly dry pond. Three cinnamon-colored bears had come to visit (a sow and two cubs). As I was making this discovery Piccolo also noticed the bears. Her head went up, she stared for a moment, then started moving down meadow. She stopped to graze on the way, but her progress, although casual, was steady. The cubs spooked into the timber as the horse approached, but the sow moved only to the bank where she sat waiting. When the horse stopped at the shore to graze, the sow returned to her digging. One of the cubs returned to dig near its mother. Again I tried to see a hump or a dished face, but couldn't be certain. Piccolo grazed near the bears until they left the meadow, an amazing sight!

October 9, 1987

The bears are down meadow again. All look golden when backlit by the bright sun. Today all three dug for the yampa roots on the pond. I had been sitting on the fence watching the family for some time when my friend Cal drove in. Cal, who is more knowledgeable about bears than I, studied the sow carefully, then said that she was unquestionably a grizzly. While her hump is not large and it is difficult to see her dished face when looking against the bright sun, her configuration is typical of a grizzly. I must speak to Piccolo about hobnobbing with such companions. We spent a delightful afternoon watching this family of bears as they foraged for food. Now I wonder if this isn't the same female I watched earlier in the summer near the south end of my property.

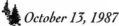

October 13, 1987

The cubs and their mother spent about an hour this afternoon digging in the bed of the pond down meadow. For a time the sow worked in an area of shade. In that light both her hump and her dished face were easily seen. The bears worked steadily except for one brief interruption; the sow raised to her hind legs and looked about in all directions. Impressive! Humbling! I feel certain, now, that the bear seen with twin cubs on July 1, 1985, is the same grizzly that I have watched on four occasions in 1987.

I prefer the company of bears. But in this valley even a "loner" like me will find people to love, to appreciate and enjoy, to laugh with or at, to tolerate or possibly to actively dislike. I learned that even in these hills one finds humor in unexpected places.

In July of 1974 the treasurer of Missoula County wrote me the following: "On January 10, 1966 county check #24933 for $5 was issued to you. Please cash it so that we can clear our books." I wrote that lady that I held no such check, nor did I recall ever having received it. I regard her next letter as a minor classic! I was told that since I did not have the check, I was to report at the courthouse in Missoula (a drive of 180 miles), take out an indemnity bond for twice the size of the check ($10), then report to the County Treasurer who would issue me a new check for $5. It was as simple as that. In my reply I suggested that I was forced to reject her kind offer. Somehow a drive of 180 miles plus the forfeiture of $10 to recover the $5 due me, seemed to set me up as loser in this game of finance. I suggested that she continue to hold the money as she had been doing for the past eight years.

The response from the county bureaucracy seemed conciliatory. The next envelope contained a partially completed indemnity form. I was told to take this form, together with two sponsors who could swear that I was worth $10 over and above just debts, to a notary, then return the properly executed form to her. She would then issue a new check to me. The correspondence stopped when I wrote that even if I were able to find the sponsors as she suggested, I felt that the effort required and the time involved, precluded the action. Since the check was never re-issued I can only assume that by some special dispensation the books were closed without returning the money due to me. The county conscience was clear; after all, they had tried. I might add that I harbor them no ill will. The story has been well worth the sum sacrificed.

Other people encounters have also given me fodder. One day I met a mounted madman on the trail in Holland Canyon. We had spent a rewarding day in the hills and were traveling down the canyon trail at a good clip when I heard horses behind me. Because of a steep drop on my right and an equally steep climb on my left I couldn't leave the trail to allow the horses to pass. Without looking back I barreled on to the switchback where I stepped off the trail just ahead of a somber-looking rider and his two-horse string. I had barely made it; both dogs were swept down the trail ahead of the horses. Later, either through error or design, this chap appeared behind me again. This time the trail wasn't rocky, so the sounds made by the horses' hooves were muffled. I didn't realize how close they were until I heard a voice snarl, "Get off the trail or I'll run you down." I turned, found a horse's head at my shoulder, and in the next instant was knocked off the trail. I landed on my feet, and cursed. The chap should have been well ahead of me and leaving the canyon by this time. This man seemed to harbor an intense dislike for backpackers. I feel certain that he was either drunk or is mentally ill, probably a bit of both. One may meet a bully anywhere, but a bully on horseback has the advantage.

August 18, 1977

Our climb to Pony Lake on the western face of the Swan Range was routine. We stopped at the lake for only a moment, then took an off-trail climb to the divide between Pony and Cat lakes. I love the drop to the lake from this point. The Cat basin is small, wooded except in its highest parts, and quiet. We had enjoyed ourselves, dropping slowly, stopping frequently to look about, and were only a short distance above the lake when I heard the first blast of gunshot. Christ! What moron would carry a gun into this sanctuary? Then there were five more shots in quick succession. My bellow must have matched the gunshots in volume of sound. I couldn't see the person shooting. Which way was he aiming? There was a period of silence. The person below me was probably as surprised by my outburst as I had been by the shooting. Then I heard one final shot, the gunman's way of telling me to go to hell. Some folks, I suspect, are afraid to hike far into the hills without carrying a gun for protection. After they arrive at their destination they feel they must use it. Since I was coming to this lake for the peace and solitude

I'd always found there, a solitude which I was unwilling to share with the trigger-happy folks below me, we started our climb back up the mountain.

Another shock awaited me in the valley. At the post office I learned of a fire on the mountain at Rumble Creek. My God—the blaze would be about three miles from the cabin, and much closer to the Berners' cabin. I raced home, turned the horses into the lower meadow to feed, then drove to Dave and Caroline's. I found them, hoses connected and waiting, watching the fire on the mountain above them. One small plane darted in and out of the smoke as it directed much larger planes that were dropping a flame-colored retardant on the blaze. Smoke jumpers, leaping from other planes, drifted to earth on large, orange parachutes while gear (chain saws, axes, shovels, and food) floated downward on white parachutes. The entire spectacle was both new and exciting to me. At intervals, fire raced up the mountain in the crowns of trees from the central area of smoke. Finally the sound of chain saws told us that the crews on the ground were now in action. We were happy to have them on our team.

Later, since we wouldn't be certain what changes the down drafts of evening might bring, I left my friends with their treasures loaded in the bed of my pickup. I carried a small amount of cash, an attractive antique bowl, and an exquisitely done, massive wood carving of grizzly bears. I carried no sterling, no gold, no diamonds, and no furs. What kind of folk are these friends of mine?

I have another story to tell about these friends. Caroline and David were settling into bed when they heard something shoot down the chimney of their propane toilet. One of their flying squirrels must surely be in trouble. When they lifted the lid of the toilet bowl to check, the fan started. They could see the squirrel standing below in a miniature tornado, but they were unable to reach it. They couldn't stop the fan because if they closed the lid of the toilet to do so the little beast would be cremated. Dave tried to unscrew the chimney without success. As he stood there wondering if he should saw through the metal pipe, Caroline had an idea. She wondered if the flyer would climb a rope if one were dropped down the chimney. So Dave trudged down to the barn for a ladder and rope. After threading the rope down the chimney both stood back to watch. It took some time, but eventually the squirrel did appear, cloaked in ash. Without hesitation it dropped to the roof, then shot off into the timber as if pursued. Its actions indicated that it had had its fill of high winds in ash-filled chimneys.

One last tale of people in this place. Locals tell the story of a "going away party" given for one of the valley's older residents. This old gentleman, who lived alone, passed away one evening while sitting at the dinner table. Later that evening one of his drinking buddies arrived with a bottle. The visitor, who was rarely sober, thought a party was in order and called in other friends. It was approaching the midnight hour when someone living nearby, puzzled by the blazing lights, went to investigate. He found his dead neighbor still sitting at the table and a party in progress. Only then was the deputy notified and the coroner called. . . . Unusual as this "sendoff" might have seemed to some, I suspect that the deceased might have approved.

Chapter Five

THE DEER

One year, winter logging in the section west of my border attracted deer from great distances. The animals heard the chain saws and came to browse on nutritious moss that hangs from branches of conifers in this part of the West. Each morning, when the loggers appeared for work, part of the herd—sometimes as many as thirty deer satiated by a night's browsing—filed quietly through my meadow toward the timber on the east. In springtime, although the loggers had been gone for weeks, many deer remained. They came to lick the mineral blocks and stayed to browse in the meadow. I met them on my walks or saw them while working about the place.

During a mild, "open" winter, deer tend to remain near my cabin through the season. When winter is severe with deep snow and bitter cold, the animals move out, congregating in groups on certain winter feeding grounds. In these deer yards, the snow is well-packed; by springtime browse is in short supply. When the deer return to my property in the spring after such severe weather, they gather quietly at the mineral blocks. As their conditions improve with better browse, the animals become less tolerant of their neighbors. When a dominant animal feels that it is being crowded at the block, it frequently raises a foreleg and strikes the offending animal standing near it. Some smaller deer are not allowed at the block until larger animals have finished there. Browsing in spring can be serious business.

Until their physical conditions improve, the deer have little time for play. But the urge to play seems to be an overpowering impulse that the animals cannot resist. At times, the first sign that group play will start soon is the sight of a young deer with dancing legs but a muzzle that is still glued to the ground. A night or two later real play begins. There is a certain sameness to this play, yet always a freshness, something different to see. Night after spring night, in the early years, I sat near the cabin watching these animals in the meadow. Just as there are certain books or concerts one remembers, so there are nights of deer play I shall never forget. The most frequent and the most spectacular periods of group play took place in 1967 and 1968, probably because there were more deer then.

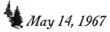 *May 14, 1967*

      Five deer play madly in the meadow. They run, they leap, they buck. They run in and out of the pond splashing water over a mallard pair that shows no concern when the deer run near, yet if I were to walk in the meadow the ducks would leave. When a small yearling walked toward the ducks, its head lowered with its muzzle almost touching the water, the ducks retreated only a short distance. When the play finally ended, all deer moved up meadow to browse.

The Deer

🌲 *May 17, 1967*

Nine deer are browsing in the meadow tonight, the proper ending for a beautiful day. Each animal, as it arrives in the meadow, goes to the block. It licks the mineral then frolics up the side of the pond to browse. Two young bucks, playing wildly near the block, swerved to avoid a large buck walking slowly toward them with his head held low in a challenging manner, but didn't miss a step in their game. Later, when these three walked up meadow, I saw antlers about six inches long on the big buck. These antlers, as well as the nubbins on the two smaller animals, were covered with velvet. There was much running through the water tonight. Again a mallard pair on the water ignored the playing deer even though at times they seemed to be in the deer's path.

🌲 *April 9, 1968*

The dogs and I returned from our walk just as the sun was setting over the Missions. Eighteen deer browsed quietly in the lower meadow. The setting sun brought color to the sky and the snow-covered peaks. The moon, about half full, was just appearing above the Swans. As I stood watching the deer, a mallard pair left the pond behind the cabin, circled between the moon and me, then headed north. Later, when bellies were full, the deer began to play. Ten deer chased, leaped, and dodged. Piccolo, the two-year-old mare, then started her own show in the upper meadow. This graceful animal ran along the rail fence with feet lifted high, tail raised, and nose reaching for the sky. A pair of mallards flew in from the west, circled above us, and landed on the pond down meadow. All this action played before a backdrop of the snow-covered Mission Range and the brilliantly tinted red clouds above it.

The Deer

May 12, 1968

There are eight deer in the meadow tonight, six of them involved in some of the wildest play I've seen this season. They played "follow the leader" at a mad pace, "baseball" with neither ball nor bat, and they ran through the water splashing geese as they sat on the pond watching. Later, during a period of mad play in the meadow, two geese walked out of the water and stood in the meadow among the madcap deer.

Of all the evenings of deer play two stand out in my memory, the first because of its uniqueness, the second because of its aura of sheer madness.

May 9, 1968

Two Canada geese have just walked out of the water and are feeding in the lower meadow near a doe and her twin fawns of last season. After a long period of browsing, one of the yearlings seemed to notice the geese for the first time. Slowly, then, it moved toward them, stopping to stare from time to time. As the deer cautiously moved forward, the geese slowly waddled away. The other twin became interested; both animals walked slowly toward the geese, noses to the ground as if following a scent on the grass. Then the deer lost interest and went back to browsing.

More deer arrived in the meadow. There was a short period of play after which most of the deer returned to browsing, but the doe and her twins renewed their interest in the geese. Slowly they drove the birds back into the pond. One of the yearlings followed the geese into the water, but when it turned to walk back into the meadow the geese followed. This became a game, then, fun for both deer and geese.

I left the window for a moment. When I returned it was obvious that something unusual was happening in the meadow. Two geese, waddling in their flat-footed way, moved side by side. Following them were four deer walking in single file with equal spaces between them. Dignity was maintained until the marchers had gone halfway around the pond, then it seemed that the deer could no longer tolerate such seriousness. They leaped into the air, kicking their heels about the protesting geese as they drove them into the water for the last time this evening.

 June 8, 1968

The evening would be a pretty one even if six deer weren't playing wildly down meadow. Two large bucks, their coats red and their antlers covered in deep velvet, browsed quietly near the cabin. Suddenly the largest and most stately of the bucks stopped eating. He stared for a time toward the playing deer, then stepped out with a few tricky steps, bucked two times, and started down meadow. Both animals walked into the water, drank, then stood watching the playing deer whose ranks had been swelled by the addition of seven new members. When the two bucks bounded out of the water and joined in the games, the play became manic. This period of fun ended with wild chasing, leaping, bucking, running through the water, and into and out of the timber. Some of the deer leaped into the air, then made half turns before landing on their feet, headed in the opposite direction.

I sat spellbound near the cabin, afraid to move closer for fear that any movement on my part might stop the action in the meadow. Penny, the elkhound, had no such inhibitions. She had walked to the meadow fence where she lay watching the play with interest.

There was also that lucky day when I watched two young fawns at play.

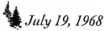 *July 19, 1968*

I had stopped the horse and sat in the saddle looking out over the valley at the Mission Range. The day was lovely; the scene seemed unusually beautiful in the morning light. Then I noticed that Piccolo seemed to be watching something in the clearcut area below us. Twin spotted fawns gamboled there, completely oblivious to the watchers above them. One fawn led as the twosome ran, high-stepped in circles, made awe-inspiring leaps and aerial twists, then played hide-and-seek in the brush. After a long period of play they started browsing.

I looked about, then, trying to locate the doe; I knew that she must be nearby but couldn't see her. When I climbed out of the saddle, however, thinking I'd give Piccolo a chance to graze, the doe blew loudly from the timber. I looked toward the sound, found the doe, then turned back to the fawns. They had been warned by their mother and were hidden now. The doe continued her warnings at intervals, and, although I waited for some time, the fawns didn't reappear. I was tempted to ride across the clearcut to search for the beauties, but decided that what I had seen had been a privilege. To ask for more would be greedy. I climbed back on the horse and we continued on down the mountain.

Might a fawn display a sense of humor? At about noon on one bright day in the middle of July we rounded a bend and found a doe with her small, spotted fawn standing in the road ahead. For a moment both animals stared at the approaching vehicle. Then the doe bounded into the timber on one side of the road, the fawn leaping toward the trees on the other. But before it reached the timber the fawn turned to look back at us. This handsome youngster stood quietly for a moment, then raised its head as high as it could and stared. I had the feeling that it was standing on tiptoes and looking down at us. The little beauty then shifted its forelegs apart, bent slightly at the knees, and lowered its head until its chin almost rested on the ground. With its eyes rolled upward, it watched us from below. The little showoff had still more tricks to show us. For a moment it stared directly at us, then suddenly turned its head and looked away as if watching something in the forest. Just as suddenly it looked back at us again, trying to catch one of us in movement. I have seen adult animals, both deer and elk, try the same maneuver on many occasions. Finally, the youngster crouched as if intending to hide. Realizing that it had no brush to drop behind, it bounded into the timber.

For some time after our arrival in the valley, my horses showed both an interest in and an intolerance toward other animals in their meadow. One evening, just before sundown, I saw that a small doe browsing in the meadow with the horses had permitted Piccolo to approach her. The filly is a curious animal. When I noticed them she was sniffing the head, neck, and shoulders of the apprehensive doe. Suddenly the deer blew loudly at the horse, then bolted. All three horses ran after the doe as she bounded from the meadow.

Over the years the horses have become accustomed to deer, just as deer now pay little attention to the horses. Some deer even show tolerance toward me. Once when I called the horses from the meadow I found them in a negative mood; they refused to come to my whistle. Damn! I started down meadow, wondering if my presence would spook a doe licking at the block. For a time confusion reigned. As the horses charged about the meadow with tails flying, the dog ran behind them, barking with unrestrained enthusiasm. My own loud curses added to the din. After the horses had run at last to the barn, I thought again of the doe. I found her standing at the block, seemingly relaxed as she calmly watched me close the gate.

One morning in late summer as I drove to the creek with tank and water pump, a doe with twin spotted fawns spooked near the north border of the property and ran into the timber. All three were back in the same area when I returned from the creek. They spooked again, but this time after running a short distance, the fawns stopped to look back at me. I turned off the motor and sat watching them. They were beautiful creatures and since they seemed to have no intention of moving on, I started talking to them. I warned them of the approaching hunting season. I told them that they must never stop to look at anyone as they were looking at me. They stood listening to me with apparent interest. Neither bounded away until I started the motor again. A few days later I saw them again in the same place. This time all three stopped to watch and stayed to listen. They are a most attractive threesome. It bothers me to think that some day they may meet someone with a gun.

In this country carelessly watched dogs, singly or in packs, can be a menace to deer. Often, a dog will instinctively chase an animal that runs from it. When we arrived here both Waif, my golden retriever, and Penny, the young elkhound, chased deer even though both knew they would be beaten for doing it. The elkhound was the most intractable. Eventually both dogs seemed to have been convinced that running deer wasn't a healthy sport for them to be involved in. One day in June of 1966 my friend Penny lay in front of the cabin watching two deer as they slowly browsed toward her in the upper meadow. When the deer had moved "dangerously" close, she stood, turned her back to the oncoming animals, then lay down again. The deer looked up from browsing, seemed to see the dog for the first time, turned, and with flags raised high-stepped back down meadow. Only then did Penny yield to what must have been a great temptation. She stood, looked toward the retreating deer, and barked.

I had another reason to be proud of Penny's response to her "don't chase" training one day as we walked back to our worksite after lunch. Suddenly I saw the dog stiffen, her hackles rising. Penny was watching a doe that ran toward us; racing behind the deer was a black dog. Although I was concerned that under the circumstances my friend might start to run the deer, I said nothing. The doe ignored us as she passed within ten feet of us. Penny quietly watched her as she passed, then charged the oncoming dog. As the weary doe slowed her pace, Penny—barking furiously—drove the black dog back in the direction from which it had come.

June 23, 1968

Much of my working day was spent burning slash in a cutover area south of the cabin. During the morning I had heard a deer blow in the brush near us on several occasions, but when I looked I could see no deer. When we returned to the fire after lunch I heard the deer again. It blew loudly many times. For a time I stood quietly looking toward the source of the sound, trying to locate the animal. Penny, who had walked to the fire site with us, had wandered off in the brush. For some time I saw nothing, then the doe jumped a log at the end of the cutover area. Beautiful!

I was still glassing the spot, hoping that a second deer would appear, when my friend Penny jumped the same log. Damn, is that dog chasing deer again? Neither dog nor doe had been traveling fast, yet I was furious. I called and whistled, but got no response. Since walking through the cutover area was difficult for either dog or man because of slash littering the ground, I started walking toward its border where traveling would be easier.

Just at that moment I saw Penny trotting along the edge of the clearcut toward me. Good dog! Then, to my surprise, I saw the doe walking behind her. Penny made a sharp turn toward me; the doe made the same turn. Penny joined Waif and me but the doe stopped a few feet from us. The deer studied me for a moment, then slowly moved off into the timber. Penny had been playing with this doe, an animal who obviously trusted the dog more than she trusted me! I smiled. When I arrived in the valley an old-timer explained to me that a dog that chased deer should be shot. Once they started chasing deer no dog could be broken of the habit, he said.

Not for several years did I learn that the act of running deer isn't always initiated by the dog. One evening in July of 1972 I was reading in the cabin when I heard a deer's loud blowing. The animal stood on the hillside across the pond, looking over at the cabin, stomping nervously with a front foot, and blowing repeatedly. I wondered at the time if she might be looking over at the white dog who lay asleep at the back door. Finally, the doe ran up the hill and disappeared among the trees at the top. I returned to my book. A short time later I again heard a deer blowing, but this time the animal sounded much closer to the cabin. The doe had skirted the end of the pond, climbed the hillside, and now stood near the cabin. Again, she was blowing and stomping as she stared at Misty. The Samoyed had ignored the doe when she stood across the water, but now the animal was much too close to the cabin to be ignored. The dog charged after the doe as she bounded away with flag waving. Although I agreed that this deer deserved to be chased, I didn't want my white friend to do the chasing. Misty came to me when I called.

While encounters of this kind are not frequent, they do continue to occur. It seems that when the season is right for an easy run some deer invite a good chase.

June 25, 1973

Misty stood in the meadow tonight watching a young doe as she walked toward the block. The doe stopped moving, turned, and stared at the dog. For just a moment the two animals stood watching one another. Then, with her flag up, the doe deliberately high-stepped toward the dog. This dare the Samoyed could not resist; as the doe bounded away the white dog charged after her. When I whistled my friend trotted back to the cabin.

May 16, 1974

As we walked along an old logging road tonight we happened upon a large buck. Misty, who was in the lead, stopped moving and stood watching the deer. I too had stopped. For a time the animals stared at one another then, since the dog didn't move, the buck took several deliberate steps toward her. That did it; the chase was on! I whistled. When the dog trotted back to me, the buck, whose three-inch antlers were in thick velvet, stopped too and stood watching us. Not until we started moving again did the buck bound away.

In 1987 I watched Frosty, the six-year-old son of Misty, respond to a similar challenge. I had gone in the barn to feed Piccolo; Frosty lay on a patch of snow nearby. Suddenly a doe browsing not far from the dog faced him, her body tense, and her eyes unblinking. With mouth closed tightly, she blew through her nose at regular intervals. With each blast she stomped the ground with forefoot. When Frosty didn't glance her way she turned, raised her flag, and high-stepped, slowly and deliberately, away from him. When he still showed no interest she moved closer, then resumed the blowing and the stomping. Her child stood watching this display but made no move to join in the demonstration. The dog ambled into the barn to see what was keeping me. Even though he lay in the doorway the doe lost interest and resumed her browsing. Then, to my surprise, her fawn began its display. I had never seen an animal not yet a year old do this. Although its blowing was less strident and its stomping less forceful, the fawn had learned its lesson well. Not until we moved out of the barn and walked toward them did mother and child leave the meadow.

The harsh sounds made by a blowing deer can be heard for great distances. This sound indicates to me that the ani-

mal is nervous, that it is concerned about something it has
seen or heard which it doesn't understand. Usually the blowing is repeated several times. The deer is alert. It stands stiffly,
looking toward the area it is concerned about, a front leg
lifted and bent at the knee. Usually the deer slowly taps the
ground with the front foot. The sound of blowing may startle
a person if the deer is unseen and close by, yet this is a sound
I love to hear. On one occasion I approached a browsing doe
slowly, freezing in position every time she looked up at me.
When I stood about ten feet from her she became nervous,
then blew loudly four times. Her pose was rigid, her mouth
closed and head still. The blast of air that escaped from the
nose was loud and harsh. She then left the area, walking
with slow, deliberate steps, her tail flag raised.

Each spring I hope that it will be my good fortune to happen upon a fawn. These youngsters are so small, so beautifully formed and colored, and appear to be so helpless that
one cannot help but fall in love with them. My first encounter with a fawn occurred one day in late June. We'd come
up over a rise and found a tiny, spotted fawn standing unsteadily in the road ahead. It stood for a moment watching
the pickup, then slowly climbed the bank at the side of the
road and disappeared in the high weeds. The tops of the
weeds were still swaying as I parted them. The little guy lay
curled in a bed of green, its big brown eyes looking up at me,
showing no sign of fear. The eyes themselves didn't move,
but as I watched, the lids slowly closed and remained closed
as if in true sleep. I stood there watching the fawn for several minutes, then looked about for the doe. She must have
been nearby, but she was well hidden. I tiptoed down the

bank and drove away. On our return a short time later, we met a doe with a fawn of similar size not far from the original encounter. The bed in the weeds was empty.

In twenty years I've not seen a doe drop a fawn, but on June 17, 1972, I don't think I missed the birth by more than a few minutes. It was a beautiful morning. Moisture glistened on trees and brush following rain during the night. Piccolo, in a near placid mood, provided only minor irritations on the ride this morning. I was euphoric as we turned down toward the cabin from the Y. Then I saw the doe as she stood in the brush a few feet off the road. She didn't spook even though man, horse, and dog had appeared suddenly and were standing near her. This girl stood in a semi-squat position, her rear toward us, her head and shoulders turned so that she looked directly at us. Misty, who was a short distance ahead, was not looking at the doe. With her forefeet up on the bank, the dog was showing great interest in something that lay hidden in the brush. I nudged the horse ahead. The fascinated dog stood with her nose about two feet from a tiny, newborn, spotted fawn that lay curled in the brush at the roadside. The big brown eyes of this little beauty looked up at us without concern. Although Misty couldn't have been better behaved, it seemed unreasonable to expect that such behavior would continue indefinitely. I nudged the horse, called the dog, and we moved on. At the sound of my voice the doe bounded away. With Piccolo in her stall and Misty safely shut in the cabin, I jogged back up the hill with the camera. The fawn had been moved, of course. I searched the area for any sign of placenta or membranes and found none. (I've learned since that time that the doe usually eats

these remnants.) I am confident that we surprised this doe
either in the delivery of the placenta or of a twin fawn.

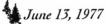 *June 13, 1977*

When we rounded a bend in a logging road today, we
came upon a mule deer doe with twin fawns standing in
the road ahead. The doe stood looking at us for a moment, then turned and walked rapidly up the road followed by the wobbly-legged little beauties that tried to
match her pace. When the three animals had disappeared
around a curve in the road we started moving again. We
found no doe when we turned the same curve, but the
young ones were there waiting for us. They milled about,
letting us approach slowly and showing no sign of nervousness.

I stopped the Jeep about twenty feet from them and
to my surprise both fawns then started walking toward
us. Thinking better of this they hesitated, then stopped
moving. As they stood looking at us, they slowly opened
and closed their toothless jaws, nuzzled each other, and
acted as if being the center of attention was just another
everyday occurrence. These little fellows were perfectly
formed. Their bodies, a little smaller than that of my
Samoyed friend, were dark rust in color, dotted with large
spots of subdued yellow. Their eyes were huge, their ears
large and erect. Their tails were small with black tips.

After some moments of indecision, both fawns moved
to the brush-filled ditch where they lay down. It was at
this point, when the master was filled to bursting with
mother-love, that Charlie, daughter of Misty, either
jumped or was pushed from the cab of the Jeep. God!
The dog charged to the roadside, stopped, and stared at
the helpless fawns. I shouted! I cursed! With the dogs

safely shut in the cab I walked to the roadside so that I too might view these lovely children. I could detect no movement of either chest wall or the eyelids in either fawn. One fawn lay on its side in the brush. Its eyelids were open. The other fawn hadn't quite made it to the prone position. It kneeled at the side of its sibling, on forelegs which were bent at the knees. Its hind legs were straight and its body was on a slant. The head had been rotated so that the left eye, which was open but unseeing, looked upward. Either figure might well have been a creation of bronze by Charley Russell.

For some time I stood watching, then turned and walked slowly back to the Jeep. The fawns didn't react in any way to the moving vehicle as we passed them. I stopped a short distance up the road, turned off the motor, and waited to see if the doe would collect her youngsters. We didn't stay long because I knew that anything I might see could only be an anticlimax.

One bright spring morning as I walked on a game trail across a high, timbered ridge I was startled by a loud, piercing cry. Charlie and Frosty, who had been at my side a moment before, had discovered a tiny, spotted fawn standing near a large serviceberry bush about ten feet from us. I called the dogs, then heard the doe blowing in the timber. With the dogs at my side, we moved slowly toward the fawn. Beneath very large ears the little guy wore the uncomprehending expression one finds in the very young. Its coat was reddish and its spots were light yellow. For a time as I glassed it from a distance the fawn stood quietly, then sank to its knees in front. I suppose it had been about to lie down but found its movements limited by the nearness of the bush. Because of the crowding, its hind legs remained straight. We slowly walked around the newborn and went on our way, leaving the child in its mother's care.

It is said that newborn and very young fawns have no odor. For this reason the fawn is not readily found by a predator during its first few days of life. This lack of odor probably explains Charlie's confusion one day in mid-June as we walked through a cutover area on our daily check of ponds. I watched her as she trotted off into the brush, head extended and nose busily trying to find the scent of something lying there. She backed away, then approached the same area from another direction. Obviously, she was puzzled. I called the dog, then with binoculars ready, moved slowly toward the place that had interested her. I stopped moving when the head of a small spotted fawn appeared above the brush. As I gaped, the beautiful little one stood up. The fawn, probably not a day old, stood unsteadily on the rough ground. A second head appeared. When this second little fawn staggered to its feet, it lost its footing and fell against its sibling, almost knocking it down. What a picture! I stood fascinated as they shuffled about, gradually becoming more accustomed to being upright. They looked around with unseeing eyes, showing no interest in their visitors. We left them then and wandered on to check the pond. When we returned the fawns had moved. They were lying down again; I could see only their heads above the brush. With great reluctance I led the dogs back to the cabin.

Not until fawns are much older do the does bring them to the mineral blocks. On a cold morning in late June, though, I sat on the shore of a pond watching a doe, followed by her tiny spotted fawn, walk along the shore. Although this mother seemed to make no concession to the size of her child as they traveled, the distance between them remained constant. When the doe jumped a fallen trunk, which I could see above the brush, I felt certain that the fawn would be forced either to crawl under or to walk around. The little guy stopped, sized up the obstruction, prepared to leap, then cleared the trunk by a wide margin. Finally, mother and child disappeared among the trees; the show was over.

On another occasion, again from the saddle, I saw a doe standing in the barrow pit with her tiny, spotted fawn. The doe seemed unconcerned as we approached. The fawn watched quietly, too, until we must have seemed too large and much too close as we loomed above her. Suddenly, the spotted beauty crouched, although there was no brush of any height for it to hide behind. The fawn maintained her crouching position until we were well down the road, then walked to the side of her mother and started nursing.

Single births, or twins, are the general rule with deer, but on occasion I have seen a doe with triplets.

July 7, 1967

Early this morning I found a doe in the meadow with three spotted fawns. A yearling followed the foursome as they walked to the block, but at the block she was driven off by the doe. Later these deer walked up meadow to browse. When the fawns started to play, the yearling tried to play with them. The mother of three, on several occasions, tried to drive this young deer from the meadow, but with no success. When the doe and her fawns left the meadow the yearling left with them. Was this doe trying to drive her child of last season from the family group?

The Deer

July 13, 1967

Today as I oiled the logs of the cabin I heard a splashing in the pond below. Three spotted fawns romped in the water; they leaped, they turned in the air as they do on land, and they bucked. While the small fry played in the water, the doe busied herself at the block. I saw no yearling with them today.

July 26, 1967

I find my doe and her triplets at the block across the pond. The yearling is with them again today, apparently no more welcome than she was a few days ago. When the doe strikes at her with her front feet the yearling walks away, but she never goes far. One of the fawns loitered at the block for some time after the others had climbed the hill. Later, it slowly browsed after them.

February 20, 1968

There is little snow now and large areas of the meadow are bare. I was delighted today to see that my doe and her triplets made it safely through the hunting season. They browsed for a time near the cabin. One youngster was bombastic, running, leaping, and bucking about the browsing doe. A second fawn played a bit too, but not so wildly. The third youngster browsed quietly.

April 13, 1969

Early in the evening four deer appeared at the block down meadow. I paid little attention to them until they wandered up meadow to browse. One, an older doe, was obviously pregnant. Three yearlings with her were all of the same size. If, as some authorities believe, the average doe raises young successfully only every other year, could this be the doe of 1967 still traveling with her triplets?

About three years later, late in the summer, I saw young triplets again. The doe, with three fawns still wearing faint spots, appeared at the block across the pond. The youngsters seemed smaller than I would have expected them to be at that time of year. Perhaps they had been born late in the season. When the doe finished at the block and walked away, the fawns lingered at the block for a time. Then walking in single file along the shore of the pond, they followed their mother.

In mid-August of 1968 a doe came to the block with her large fawn. For a time both mother and child quietly licked at the mineral. When the fawn became restless it browsed among the trees for a time, then walked back to its mother. As human children who want attention or are bored, the fawn started misbehaving. It stood behind its mother, raised to its hind legs, and pawed its mother's rump with its forefeet. The doe continued licking quietly at the block. The youngster moved to its mother's side and again raised to its hind feet, this time pawing its parent's back and side. The doe didn't miss a lick. But when the child started to nurse, the doe reacted; she stepped over the head of her offspring, left the block, and walked from the meadow.

On another occasion in late summer, I watched a doe and her large triplets walk along the shore of the pond toward the block. Two of the fawns went to the block with their mother and started licking, but the third fawn had other ideas. This child walked to its mother's side and started to nurse. Quickly, but not gently, this mother stepped on and over the neck of the nursing fawn, then calmly returned to the block.

As with the human family, we sometimes see a fawn that

is blessed with an overprotective parent. Early one evening as a doe and her large fawn were leaving the block, they met a yearling doe as she walked out of the timber. The yearling gave mother and child wide berth as she walked to the block. The fawn looked back at the yearling, then ran to her and smelled of her genitals much as one dog may greet another. For a brief moment, I thought that the yearling was about to return the greeting, then she seemed to change her mind and drove the large fawn away. The doe, who had been watching her child, seemed to bristle. With head down she walked toward the yearling with slow, deliberate steps. The young doe ran from the meadow followed by the fawn and her mother.

In this mountain hideaway there are pictures and events that somehow avoid classification. On occasion these pictures have been disturbing. One day late in May during my first years here I saw a doe with a fractured foreleg browsing in the meadow with several other deer. Although this little deer had great difficulty in walking, at times almost falling, she didn't seem to be especially conscious of her problem. Although the leg gave her little support she seemed to have adjusted well. Surprisingly, the little doe made it through the summer without being taken by a predator. She returned to the meadow again early in the fall. Her leg, although badly deformed, now gave better support. Several times that day I saw her strike out at other deer with both front feet, driving unwanted animals from the block. I saw too how fast she could move on that crippled leg when one of the horses trotted through the timber and spooked her. It seemed that the deformity had not lessened her good looks; she had come to the meadow with a buck in tow. He was still trailing her when she walked back into the timber.

It is amusing at times to recall a few things seen and picture them as they might appear in an animated film. In one scene we see the lower meadow in the second week of March: there are many deer about the place, some at both blocks and several browsing in the lower meadow, although we can see nothing for them to eat there. The real performance of the day takes place during a late afternoon snowfall. Four deer file out of the timber, walk to the pond for water, then go to the mineral block. For a time we lose them in the falling snow. When they appear again we see them through a thin curtain of falling snowflakes. The group plays wildly, romping about and bucking, a ballet danced under subdued lighting behind a filmy curtain. One animal slips and lies on its belly in the snow. A moment later it is up and playing again. Then, two does walk along the south shore of the pond down meadow with their yearling fawns. While the young deer run about in the water, the old girls stand quietly licking one another about the head and face. . . .

The next scene in this fantasy production of mine starts during a night of the full moon. Some time during this night all hell breaks loose in my normally quiet hideaway. Coyotes sing in the meadow, the songs of coyotes come to me from the south, and Misty sings in the cabin. There is much beauty in a coyote song offered to a full moon, even when this chorus wakes one from a sound sleep. Shortly after daylight the coyotes start singing again, but from the south. A pregnant doe that is licking at the block down meadow with two yearlings hears the coyotes but does not seem concerned, even though the animals cannot be a great distance from her. She casually raises her head, looks toward the source of the sound, then turns back to the block. The two younger deer seem to pay no attention at all. When this threesome finish at the mineral, they walk slowly from the meadow. . . .

The last scene portrays a pretty little doe that has been quietly browsing near the fence dividing the meadows. Suddenly she gives a loud snort, then is seen running along the fence blowing repeatedly and reaching out to stomp with her front foot as she runs. At first this conduct is inexplicable, then we see that she is chasing a large gray cat as it races in a panic for the hay shed. When the cat disappears in the shed, the doe returns to peaceful browsing. . . .

I have enjoyed many of these isolated happenings. Early one evening in May two small spike bucks left the block and wandered up meadow to browse. They were joined in a short time by a much larger buck. For some time the three animals browsed quietly, paying little attention to one another. Then one of the smaller bucks walked to the newcomer and proceeded to sniff the large animal's head, neck, nose, and mouth. For a brief time the large buck tolerated this examination, then exploded. With surprising suddenness he lashed out with both front feet at the curious one. All three then returned to browsing.

June 5, 1966

Late in the evening six deer came to the block down meadow. All were large animals, one of them pregnant. For a time all licked quietly at the mineral, then two of the deer walked to the pond where they stood on its shore looking toward the cabin. Suddenly both deer raised to their hind feet. Then as if on signal they turned, faced one another and started walking forward on their hind feet. When they were within striking distance both deer flailed with their forelegs as if boxing. Again, as if on signal, both animals dropped to all four feet and started browsing.

On an afternoon late in June, as I cut thistles in a logged area, a large buck wearing a massive set of antlers spooked from the brush behind me. Because of the slash left on the ground the animal was forced to carry his head low and was unable to gain speed in his run. For some unaccountable reason as I watched this boy's labored progress, I thought of a heavy man, wearing a large cowboy hat, trying to run with his pants down around his knees.

During those early years when I was seeing so much that was new and interesting to me, I never tired of watching deer. To avoid being accused of anthropomorphizing, I shall not claim that some deer, like some humans, have a well-developed sense of humor. All I will say is that if I were to do some of the things I've seen deer do, it would have been my sense of humor and love of life that directed me.

One mid-April evening eight deer browsed quietly in the lower meadow, just before sunset. The scene was one of beauty and peace. As I watched, one of the smaller animals left the group and trotted daintily to the pond for water. She was about to step into the pond when a pair of mallards swam by without seeming to notice the little doe. When the mallards were gone she stepped into the water, but before drinking she stared after the retreating ducks as if puzzled by the snub she had just received. Her thirst satisfied, she looked toward the ducks again, then walked out into the meadow. Suddenly the little girl kicked up her heels, took a few rapid sidesteps, then settled back to serious browsing.

On another April evening a lone deer browsed in the lower meadow for some time. As I watched the animal walk across the meadow, I was reminded of a child who with a hop, a skip, and a jump starts off for the candy store. The small doe looked up from her browsing, turned suddenly, danced a few steps, then trotted in a half circle. Another short period of browsing was followed by intricate steps in another direction. Then with a lope followed by a sedate walk, the animal left the meadow and disappeared among the trees.

One more evening late in April we walked along a narrow, grassed-over skid road. I slowed my pace when I saw a large doe with flag raised slowly and deliberately high-stepping along the road ahead of us. Four other deer stepped out of the brush and joined her. All of the animals soon left the skid trail and disappeared behind a large boulder. For a time I lost them—then one head appeared above the rock. Soon the lone head was joined by a second. Finally, five long necks supporting five pretty heads moved slowly from side to side as these curious animals watched us from behind their boulder. Not until we started walking again did they bound away.

About six o'clock one May morning, I found a small madcap deer kicking its heels up near two Canada geese in the lower meadow. At first the geese moved only a short distance, but as the young deer became more manic they hurried to the pond, honking loudly and flapping their wings in protest. As soon as the geese were back on the water the young deer lost interest in them; it returned to browsing.

The Deer

Part of my delight in watching some of these unusual happenings in the world of the deer arises from the fact that each event has come as a complete surprise. Too, it is easy for me to feel favored since no other person has been so privileged; I have been the sole member of the audience.

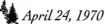 *April 24, 1970*

A doe stood at the side of the road watching Penny and me as we walked toward her. We slowed our pace. The girl's tail went up but I saw no other sign of alarm. We moved forward only a few small steps at a time. The doe leaped into the road, but instead of bounding away as I had expected her to do, she slowly high-stepped in a circle, stopping occasionally to look back at us. I stood quietly wondering what this delightfully crazy female would do next. She pranced a bit with flag elevated and stood with her back turned toward us looking around quickly from time to time to see if she might catch us moving. She danced a little and high-stepped slowly and deliberately in her circle again. We were within thirty feet of this lovely showoff. My throat began to tickle; I struggled to suppress a cough. Penny finally solved the problem by vigorously shaking her head causing her dog tags to jingle. The doe leaped from the road and disappeared among the trees. Then a smaller doe that had been hidden in the brush leaped into the road and followed the first animal into the timber.

July 24, 1980

At six this morning a very small buck stood quietly near the pond down meadow. With a suddenness which seemed almost startling to me, he stood on his hind legs, leaped into the air and in landing fell on his side. For a moment he lay quietly. Then he picked himself up and stood looking about for a time. Suddenly he leaped again, this time landing on his feet as planned. For a time he stood looking toward the cabin, then lunged to the side as if falling and trotted happily on to the block. Just a youngster doing his thing on a very large stage.

There have been many relatively minor encounters which have brought beauty to the eyes of this beholder and peace to his soul. Shortly before sundown on an evening in June as I walked toward the cabin after pelleting the horses, I noticed two buck deer near the block down meadow. One was a spike; the other wore branched antlers. Because the picture they presented was a pleasant one, I climbed the rail fence and sat watching in the sunlight. The animals browsed quietly for a time, then both looked toward the timber as a very large buck with a rack of great size walked into the meadow. As the monarch stood looking out over pond and meadow, the two smaller animals came to him and stood, one at either side. These three beautifully poised animals, their antlers in thick velvet, stood spotlighted against a dark background by the setting sun. They presented a tableau that brought a lump to my throat and moisture to my eyes.

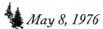 *May 8, 1976*

The early morning air felt soft and mild. I heard a hummingbird hovering about the feeder and the splash of ducks landing on the pond below. When I rounded the corner of the cabin on my way to the barn, a deer walked out of the timber and stood for a moment in the lower meadow. Suddenly, its tail went up and it lunged back toward the timber. I thought it had seen me until it did a bit of dancing, then lunged in the opposite direction. The little beauty was just feeling good; it danced all the way to the block. Then I heard the sound of wings. The mallards had taken off from the pond behind the cabin and were flying in an arc over the meadow. A rather nice start for a bright, sunny day in the mountains.

The beauty and power of a deer leaping through space remain etched in one's memory, especially if the animal was close at hand. The pleasurable thrill is there, but so is a transient fear.

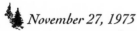 *November 27, 1973*

Late in the afternoon I wandered with Misty along an old skid road. The dog had been running ahead, investigating an odor here, a track there, but never out of sight for more than a moment or two. We left the road and climbed to a wooded ridge. I stood on a game trail studying deer tracks in the snow, breathing the good air, just feeling glad to be alive. Misty trotted to a small, wooded knoll nearby, disappeared behind it, then barked in great excitement. I turned to go to the dog just as a big buck, wearing an impressive rack, jumped from behind the knoll and headed directly for me. This beautiful animal didn't seem to notice me until he was only a few feet away. He made a tremendous leap, and for a moment I thought he would hit me. When he passed me his feet were at the height of my shoulders, only an arm's length away. What power in that body, what grace, what a thrill for me! Misty was roundly thumped for barking at the buck, of course, but somehow my heart was not in that thumping.

Chapter Six

THE ELK

I saw no elk my first fall and winter here. In early spring, the few animals I saw licking at the block or feeding in the meadow were less than stimulating. Somehow, I was disappointed. Finally, on a bright day in May, I met my first small herd of elk.

I had parked the Jeep on a mountain road and with the two dogs had climbed to a mountain meadow where I had hiked a few days before. Nine elk, cows and young animals, stopped eating and stood watching as I stepped from the timber into the grassy meadow. I froze when I saw them, but the dogs continued to move, investigating a scent here, a ground squirrel hole there. To my surprise the elk seemed to pay little attention to the dogs, and my friends showed no interest in the elk. The herd watched me as I slowly sank to my knees, then sat on the ground. When the dogs tired of their explorations they came and sat near me. Except for the action of my arms as I raised and lowered the binoculars, we did not move.

The elk became more curious; as a group they moved

slowly toward us. The animals were about thirty feet away when one of the cows started to circle, picked up our scent, barked loudly two times, and ran for the timber. The term "bark" seems an adequate description of the sharp sound made by the sudden expulsion of air from the mouth and nose of the elk. It can be likened, I think, to a nervous cough in humans. Both cows and bulls bark when they have seen or heard something they question. The other animals followed the cow elk as she disappeared among the trees at the side of the meadow.

Some weeks later, as Socks carried me along a high logging road, we came upon seven elk, one a small, spotted calf, in a clearcut below us. The animals had seen us before we saw them. All seven crossed the road ahead of us, climbed through a logged area, and trotted in among the trees. When they were gone, I looked back into the lower clearcut. A large calf had just walked out from behind a clump of brush. Its confusion suggested to me that it had been sleeping. I was astonished when this young animal, which still carried a few spots, climbed to the road, then trotted up the road toward us. Horse, rider, and dog were within twenty feet of the calf when it seemed to realize its error. It stared at us briefly then trotted from the road toward the trees above.

In April 1968, when I returned to the cabin after a day of work in timber, I found elk at the block down meadow. I watched them until they disappeared among the trees, then went to the barn to feed the horses. As I threw down hay from the loft, I saw that a few of the elk had returned to the mineral. I sat in the doorway to watch. The next animal to appear outside the rail fence was a young bull with long, retained spikes. Instead of jumping the fence as I'd expected him to do, he paced back and forth, chose the section of fence with the widest space between the rails, and worked his way through. I was fascinated. First he rotated his head, thrust head and spikes between the rails, then brought his head back to the vertical. Then the animal walked forward until his chest struck the lower rail. Now he brought one front leg through at a time. Again he walked forward. When his hind legs struck the lower rail he again brought one through at a time, then trotted to the block joining the others there.

More elk appeared at the fence and all worked their way between the rails in the same manner—all, that is, except one large cow. She found the space between the rails too narrow to permit her to thrust a foreleg through when her chest was against the lower rail. This cow backed out and trotted off. She must have jumped the fence somewhere out of my sight since she appeared at the block a short time later. I watched as eleven elk milled about. Six deer appeared, moved about as if studying the herd, but made no attempt to join the group. Only two elk were antlered, both were young bulls with retained spikes.

Although I sat in the doorway for quite some time, only two elk left the meadow. One leaped the fence from a standing position with ease. The other, a smaller animal, leaped between the rails without touching either rail. Then, because I was hungry and cold, I started back to the cabin. I walked where the animals couldn't see me from the meadow, thinking I'd watch them later from the warmth of the cabin. However, Waif and Penny saw me coming, barked their welcome, and spooked the elk. When I arrived at the window the animals were gone.

Two years later, again in April, the dogs and I hiked out the road during a heavy snowfall. Three elk broke out of the timber, stood in the road watching us for a time, then were gone. We waited quietly to see if more animals might appear. Twelve more elk crossed the road in single file, climbed the bank, and disappeared among the trees. The heavily falling snow, together with the complete absence of sound, gave to this encounter a dreamlike quality.

On a morning late in June I'd finished breakfast and was pouring my coffee when I saw seven elk in the lower meadow. I walked up to the fence so that I might see them better. Misty and I stood there for some time, then crawled between the rails and walked very slowly toward the elk, stopping frequently to study them. Two large, spotted calves lay sleeping until we were in mid-meadow, then they too stood and quietly watched us. Two large spike bulls grazed with the group. All the animals seemed to accept us, many turning their backs to us as they fed. Finally, as we continued to approach, they became restless. A large cow walked toward us, stared, then started barking. Even when the herd began their retreat they didn't panic, but walked slowly back toward the block. I returned to the cabin to cold coffee, but somehow I didn't mind.

As I finished my dinner one evening , I noticed that the doe I'd seen browsing in the upper meadow was no longer eating. She was intently watching something down meadow. When I checked I found several elk feeding in mid-meadow and a second group licking at the block across the pond. I had not seen so many elk in a long, long time, so I rushed out with binoculars to watch them. Eighteen elk, cows and young stuff, were wandering about down meadow. Sixteen of them eventually worked their way toward the fence between meadows where they stood watching the horses in the upper meadow. Twice when Piccolo pranced toward the fence with tail up and head held high, she put them to flight. Neither time did the elk run far. Finally, all elk walked to the corner of the meadow. Some jumped the fence from a standing position. A few walked along the fence into the timber, while one animal tried to climb between the rails without success. Some of the animals were thin, but most of them seemed to have wintered well.

Those spring days when deer and elk start their migration through the property can be delightful. The temperature one morning in the middle of April was twenty degrees and there was some breeze. The horses high-stepped about with tails held high, snorting, bucking, and farting. Shortly after dawn, as I walked toward the barn, I heard geese. Then I saw the pair as they sailed in over the trees and landed. A little later elk walked out of the timber and headed for the block. When all had arrived their numbers totaled twenty-one. On the pond between the elk and the cabin were two Canada geese and four ducks.

I was away for a time in the afternoon, but when I returned all twenty-one elk were back in the meadow. Two of the animals had spikes retained from last season. Seven stood in the water looking toward the cabin. The rest either lay on the residual patch of snow on the south side of the water or stood near the block. From time to time some of the animals changed their positions, but there was little actual movement of the herd. Occasionally, one animal prodded another to its feet. Finally, a few at a time, they wandered off into the timber.

About a month later there were elk in the meadow again. The meadow was green; the animals were more sleek in appearance after a month of good eating. Four stood in the pond, posing as though placed there by an artist. A couple of mallards swam quietly a short distance from the legs of one of the posing elk.

Not until the sexual urge strikes the older bulls in the fall do they start collecting their harem. This is the season for bugling and for fighting. I've seen no fighting—which, of course, proves nothing—nor have I heard bugling here in the valley. Bulls bugle across the mountains in the Bob Marshall Wilderness and in Glacier National Park to the north; there should be no reason for them to be mute here. Yet I've heard none of these delightful, stimulating sounds of the rut in the Swan Valley. The appearance of cows with spotted calves in early summer would indicate, I think, that the herd here is not without its sex life.

When I glanced out at six one morning in June, I found a large bull at the block. His massive antlers were in velvet. Two smaller bulls walked out of the timber and approached the block. The smaller of the newcomers was allowed to lick mineral, the other was not. Whenever the larger of the two young bulls approached the block, he was checked either by the body of the large bull or by his antlers. These sensitive antlers were not used carelessly; on occasion this big bull lowered his head and walked toward the animal he was threatening.

When I walked to the barn to feed the horses only the large bull was to be seen. He turned his back to me as I opened the gate, ignored the horses as they charged into the meadow, then continued to ignore them as they grazed toward him. When Penny barked her greeting as I returned to the cabin, the antlered one looked our way for a moment, then casually turned back to the block.

Early in the season when an antlered bull stands in the shade at the block, it may be difficult to see its antlers, even though they may be long and branched. At this time of year the antlers are covered with a velvet that is so thick and so brown in color it matches the hair on the ears of the animal. Only when the bull moves into the sunlight can one see the antlers clearly.

The shedding of winter hair begins early in summer. In mid-June one year, two three-point bulls left the block and walked up meadow toward me. One animal had completely shed his winter hair; his coat was bright and attractive. The other bull still carried a good bit of dull, faded hair on his back, shoulders, and rump. Although I stood only a short distance from them, both animals lay down in the high grass. There they continued to eat until they could no longer reach grass by stretching their necks, then they lay contentedly chewing their cuds. Several times these bulls looked directly at me, but neither animal showed concern.

On an evening in mid-June I sat for some time watching two bull elk as they grazed in the lower meadow. Shortly before dusk the largest bull of the evening walked out of the timber, grazed with the other two bulls for a short time, then wandered up meadow toward me. He was a beauty; he carried a huge rack of six points. His sole interest seemed to be Piccolo, the young mare, as she ran wildly back and forth on the other side of the fence. Although I had by now climbed between the rails and stood in the meadow a short distance from him, he paid no attention to me. The bark of an unseen elk across the fence to the west caused him to look that way for several minutes. He turned, then, and with very deliberate steps trotted back down meadow.

One evening late in June of the following year I was putting up the bars in the meadow gate after giving the horses their pellets when I noticed that a large bull elk had come to the mineral block. I could see that he, too, was a six-pointer. Back at the cabin I sat on a bench watching the animal down meadow. He stayed at the block for some time, then walked to the pond for water. This bull was large, his rack huge. When he had drunk his fill he started walking sedately up meadow toward me. Suddenly, he broke his stride, took a few intricate steps, first to one side then to the other. He was a beautiful specimen, graceful in his actions and in the best of spirits. When he stood at the meadow fence he was so close to me that I could see each individual blade of grass as it dangled from his lips. We stared quietly at one another for several minutes. Then the bull barked. His bark brought the horses from the barn on the run. The sight of the charging horses spooked the bull. As he trotted into the timber at the end of the meadow, he carefully rotated his head so that his big rack would strike neither trunks nor branches.

Early in the fall of 1976, I found myself hosting a bull elk who had one broken antler. When he left the block he walked to the almost dry pond, stood in the water, and started churning the mud with his large, unbroken antler. As this didn't seem to produce the results he hoped for, he pawed with a front foot. Finally satisfied, he lay in the mud, rolled over, then lay quietly for a long time.

The following spring, as we walked out the road, Misty and Charlie trotted off into the brush. I heard Misty bark in great excitement, then heard the thudding of hooves. Four elk broke out of the timber. Three leaped into the road behind me, but one, a large spike bull with retained antlers, stopped on the bank near me. He, too, appeared to be about to leap off the bank into the road; he was headed directly for me! There was a moment's hesitation, then the leap with a slight change of direction which brought him into the road about three feet in front of me. Now the boy showed no hesitation. With a mighty leap the bull left the road and reached the bank. Two more bounds and he was in the timber. I turned, hoping to see the animals behind me. Two were already out of sight, a third, a bull with retained branch antlers, was just disappearing in the forest.

Not all elk leave the meadow when their hunger for mineral has been temporarily satisfied. Occasionally these animals decide that they like it here as they proved to me one day in June of 1978. Three bull elk were at the block when I checked the meadow about five-thirty that morning. A little later I found them browsing in mid-meadow. A cowbird flew from the ground to the rump of one of the animals. Slowly the bull turned his head. When his muzzle seemed about to touch the bird, the cowbird flew to the neck of the same animal where it remained as long as I watched. Several times during the day when I checked the meadow I found all three bulls there. Late in the evening I found them grazing near the fence between meadows. With Charlie at my side, I started moving slowly toward them. The smaller animals spooked a short distance but the largest, a four-pointer, stood his ground. He seemed to be as curious about us as we were about him. Finally, he slowly high-stepped to the edge of the timber where he turned again to stare at us. What a majestic animal that bull was, his antlers in thick, brown velvet! His curiosity satisfied, he walked to the fence, leaped with ease from a standing position, and trotted off.

On a beautiful, bright day in mid-July we'd just come out into the open after making a fairly steep climb up a timbered slope in the Missions when I sensed that the dogs were no longer with me. The next moment I heard them barking a short distance to my left. I glanced about me. To my surprise I found a large bull elk, his antlers in velvet, standing on the crest of the ridge about twenty feet above me. The animal may not have seen me — his undivided attention was directed toward the barking. His attitude seemed to be one of intense interest rather than fear, since with one forefoot raised he stared toward the source of the sound. He stood like this for some time. Then, never glancing my way, he slowly and deliberately high-stepped in an arc in front of me and moved toward the trees below. He stood at the edge of the timber for a time, still looking toward the source of the barking. Without ever having looked my way, he quietly disappeared among the trees.

I dared not move, either to photograph the elk or to call the dogs, until the bull was out of sight. After he was gone I whistled and we started walking up the ridge. I found tracks of two elk in a patch of snow higher on the ridge. The dogs had been conversing with the second elk, I'm sure. As we climbed higher I looked out into the drainage of Red Butte Creek. Far to the north I could see this creek as it cascaded down through the timber from an area of rock slabs.

We lunched on the highest point of the butte. I fed the dogs, but before starting on my own lunch I looked about for old friends in the wilderness. Most of the lakes I could see were now free of ice. All creeks were raging and I could see the water as it poured from Lake-of-the-Clouds in a good stream. From where I stood I could see only the start of the falls, but having been there I well remembered the thundering of the falls as the water landed on the valley below. After lunch we walked the butte. I was relaxed, completely at ease, and not prepared for the crash of a sonic boom which reverberated through the mountains. Those bastards! I arrived home weary, but at peace with my world. This was a day for the soul.

One day late in May I stood on a ridge above an old sawmill site on my property, looking across at newly hung birdhouses. Waif lay at my feet, and Penny lazily nosed about below. I shut my eyes trying to identify a bird song. When I opened them a few moments later I found myself looking into the eyes of a cow elk. She hadn't been in the sawmill site a moment before, at least I hadn't seen her. Where the devil had she come from? I didn't move.

The cow elk barked but was ignored by Penny. She paced warily back and forth, stopping now and then to look our way, then barked again, this time louder than before. Penny heard this bark and as I wasn't sure just what she might do,

I called to her in a low voice. She climbed the ridge and lay beside Waif. I'd expected either my voice or the sight of the moving dog to spook the elk, but she continued her pacing below, barking from time to time. We didn't move. Finally the cow climbed to the ridge on which we were sitting, stood staring at us for a time, then walked in among the trees. She was much too thin to be pregnant. I wondered if she might have a calf nearby. Later, when we dropped to the sawmill site, I found the cow still watching us from the timbered area above.

Two months later as we walked along an old grass-covered skid road near this ridge and sawmill site, a cow elk ran across the road ahead of us. Instead of disappearing in the timber as I'd expected her to do, she trotted in a wide half-circle, then waited again at the roadside for us to approach. Several times when we drew near she crashed over downfall, only to again take up her post in the lane ahead. This girl was acting like a nitwit; elk aren't supposed to do these things.

The lane we were traveling dipped into an old clearcut. As we started down the grade I saw the cow in the clearcut below. We stopped and stood watching her, just as she was watching us. The elk walked cautiously toward us, circled a bit, then just as cautiously took a few steps away from us. Suddenly she started barking. Both dogs sat quietly behind me. I moved only when raising or lowering the binocular, or when brushing mosquitoes from my face. Finally, since the elk had been standing quietly for some time, I started moving slowly toward her. She didn't spook as we approached but merely stepped aside and stood barking as we passed.

When I glanced back I found the cow walking slowly and deliberately toward the place where we had been standing. I heard barking long after I could no longer see her.

I spent one day late in July exploring in the high country with the dogs. When we returned to the cabin early in the evening, I noticed a cow elk licking at the block across the water. Her faintly spotted calf stood in the pond, drinking. The reflection of the youngster in the water was so perfect that I seemed to be watching two calves standing muzzle to muzzle. The cow worked at the block for a long time, then joined her calf in the pond. The splashing of mother and child as they walked about in the water roused two tired dogs who were sleeping at the back door. When the dogs barked the elk left the water and slowly browsed up the hillside among the trees. At dusk I found the cow back at the block across the water. Her calf lay quietly nearby.

When elk have played in the meadow, rarely, the enjoyment gained in watching them has been well worth time lost in the watching.

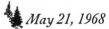 *May 21, 1968*

In the evening two bull elk came out of the timber to the block down meadow. The larger animal, a spike bull, licked at the mineral for a time, then walked to the pond. What a majestic appearance this boy presented as he stood in the water, staring at the nearby horses! Two deer, dwarfed, of course, by the size of the elk, stood at the side of the pond watching the big animal. For a time the elk stared quietly at the deer, too, then with head lowered, he walked out of the water toward them. Both deer scampered away, but they were soon back playing about the bull. Then, to my surprise, he joined them in the fun. He leaped into the air and landed, he bucked, he leaped again and made a quarter turn in the air before landing. The exhibition over, he trotted slowly back to the block.

Early one morning as I was on my way to the barn I saw a young bull elk trotting toward the block. Two deer stood watching him with interest. This chap seemed to be in good spirits since when he finished at the block and walked to the pond for water, he leaped into the air several times, made a quarter turn in the air with each leap, then continued on to the water. When the bull started his show, both deer scampered to a place of safety in the timber.

On another occasion six elk walked out of the timber and walked toward the same mineral lick. One was a large bull with antlers in thick velvet. Three of the smaller animals started to play, chasing one another with heads up and necks extended. They pranced, posed, and ran through the pond. Even the antlered bull, a four-pointer, tried to enter the game when he finished at the block. He soon decided that this play was not for him, though, and walked with dignity into the timber.

May 3, 1980

Tonight I walked to the front deck while the sun was still high above the Mission Range. The meadow was green and lovely. A Wilson's snipe, which I couldn't see, was orchestrating at a great height above me and a bluebird pair were feeding from the meadow fence. For a time I tried to read, but somehow the printed page couldn't hold my attention. I glassed the block down meadow but saw nothing. I read a bit more, then glassed again. Eight elk were now crowded about the block; three more animals were trotting out of the timber. For some time there was little real action down there. Many animals were busily licking at the block. A few stood about quietly, looking out over the meadow.

Three elk walked to the pond, stepped into the water, and drank. When they'd taken their fill the play started. These three youngsters of last year's hatch pranced about in the water, heads held high, noses angled upward, water splashing. One animal leaped into the air, bucked, then turned partially in the air before landing back in the pond with a huge splash. The other two animals then offered their versions of these tricky steps. Finally, all three left the pond, ran back and forth along the shore, in and out of the timber. The rest of the herd showed no interest in their young at play. Finally played out, one of the youngsters walked slowly up meadow. Both dogs watched the approaching elk for a time, then they decided to put the run on the cheeky beast. Both dogs stopped moving when I called. The elk turned and trotted back to the herd.

It would be unreasonable to expect that all encounters with animals in the wild would give pleasure. I drove home from getting the mail one noon early in January and found an elk bedded down in the sunlit meadow. Great! But as I looked again I wondered if it was really so great. I'd never seen elk in the lower meadow in winter. I could see few details because of the glare of bright sunlight on fresh snow. Slowly, I moved into the timber. There I was partially protected from the glare, yet could still see the elk. Something was radically wrong with this picture. The animal's muzzle was much too thin and pointed. I looked again, then decided that this elk had a beard. But elk do not have beards. Further study showed me that this "beard" contained teeth. At this point I realized that this animal had suffered a fracture of both mandibular condyles. Its beard could only be a drooping lower jaw. When I saw the tongue hanging down over the jaw and saliva glistening in the sunlight as it dripped from the mouth, I felt ill. This elk was in serious trouble; it needed help. I jumped into the Jeep and headed for the ranger station. But when I returned with my help the meadow was empty.

Alone again, I decided to investigate. If I had not been hallucinating, I should find blood-streaked sputum in the snow down meadow. I slipped on the snowshoes and started walking. Because I was giving all my attention to the spot where the elk had been lying, I did not see the animal as it stood in the timber bordering the meadow. Then I heard it move, saw it jump the fence from a standing position, and disappear among the trees. There were streaks of blood in the snow, both where the animal had been bedded in the meadow and where it had been standing in the timber. Some bastard in trying to poach an elk by spotlight had put a bullet through both mandibular condyles. The lower jaw was now useless. The injury had been a recent one; the animal's condition was good. Death by starvation would be very, very slow.

Because of flecks of blood in the snow it was possible to track the injured animal through a maze of elk tracks for a distance of about one and a half miles. In this distance the animal had bedded down two other times. The tracks disappeared at Cooney Creek; they did not reappear on the far side of the creek. The elk must have walked for some distance, either up or down the creek, before it left the water and climbed the bank. Although I made daily trips to the area, walking on snowshoes in ever widening circles on both sides of the creek, I found no tracks. Nor did I see ravens in the sky which might lead me to the dead or dying animal. This elk must have traveled a great distance before it lay down to die.

Most days, though, living as I do I am somewhat insulated from man's cruelty, his thoughtless destruction of wildlife and their habitat.

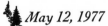 *May 12, 1977*

As I stepped out on the deck with my book tonight, five elk left the block and slowly walked through the pond to browse up meadow. I watched them from the deck for a time, then with the two dogs beside me, I moved very slowly toward the meadow fence. There I sat for a time on the top rail. These elk were beautiful animals, the largest a three-point bull with antlers in velvet. Three were cows. The fifth animal had gone back to the block.

Since none of the elk seemed apprehensive, after watching for a time I moved slowly along the fence toward them. Again I climbed and sat on the fence. Both dogs entered into the spirit of the game; they stayed at my side as we walked, then sat quietly below me when I watched from the rails. I was now probably no more than forty feet from the animals. Although they didn't seem to be disturbed by our nearness, they did look up from their grazing now and then to glance our way.

Then, for no reason that I could see, all four animals stopped grazing and walked slowly to the west meadow

fence. There the bull jumped with ease into the lane beyond. I thought the fun was over, but for reasons of their
own the cows didn't follow the bull. Soon all three cows
started grazing toward us. The bull leaped back into the
meadow and joined the cows. All four elk were grazing
near us again. When I left the fence and started moving
toward them, they slowly moved away. When we stopped
moving, they stopped and stood watching us. Finally one
of the cows spooked and all trotted back down meadow.
Each female urinated as she walked through the water of
the pond.

About nine o'clock the next evening I saw that five elk
were feeding in the meadow. The three-point bull was not
with them. They were all fine specimens, large, well-nour-
ished animals with glossy coats. Again I walked slowly toward them, but because swarms of famished mosquitoes
buzzed about my head, I didn't show the patience of the
evening before. For a time the animals fed as we approached,
then they struck graceful poses and held them. It was a striking tableau. When we started moving again, the largest cow
lost her cool; she barked as she stood looking at us, then
barked two times more. All five elk turned and trotted from
the meadow. I could hear the cow barking long after the
animals had disappeared among the trees.

Chapter Seven

FLAT-FOOTED WANDERERS

On my property, or near its borders, are twelve potholes of varying size. Most contain enough water to float ducks except in years of severe drought. These potholes have enhanced my enjoyment of the place and have furthered my understanding of things wild. Barrow's goldeneyes and mallards raise families here year after year. Other ducks nest here on occasion—hooded mergansers, ring-necked ducks, buffleheads. Less frequent visitors are cinnamon teal, green-winged teal, and shovelers. In spring a mated pair of ducks may appear on a pond when there is but a narrow strip of open water between the ice-covered surface and shore. There they may remain for an hour, or for a day or two, then are gone. Eventually a nesting site is chosen and the serious business of starting a family is begun. Mallards nest on the ground; goldeneyes nest in cavities.

Over the years I have noted and recorded the behavior of ducks on these small mountain potholes. Barrow's goldeneyes dominate the pond. Belligerence, in my experience, seems to be a characteristic quality of the goldeneye, especially when mating, nesting, or raising young. This fighting instinct can be seen in the very young.

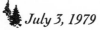 *July 3, 1979*

Two young goldeneyes, all that remain of "family three," have been alone on Pond Nine since June 22. As I walked toward this tiny pond today I heard soft quacking. This seemed strange as the young goldeneyes had never been vocal. I looked out over the pond and located the two young ducks on the water, but saw that the quacking was not coming from them. As I stood glassing that end of the pond a large mallard hen swam out of the reeds. She was followed by six partially grown youngsters. How sedately these mallards traveled as they swam near the young goldeneyes. The mallards stopped and sat quietly on the water about ten feet from the two young ducks.

When one of the goldeneyes dove I assumed it was feeding, until I saw the startled mallard hen flapping her wings and heard her loud protests. The young duck, at the advanced age of eighteen days, had made an underwater attack on an adult mallard hen, as adult goldeneyes frequently do. When the youngster swam back to its sibling it was received with the proper reassuring movements of head and neck, just as the adult drake would have been greeted had he made the attack. All was quiet on the pond for a time. Then the pugnacious youngster swam slowly toward the mallard family, its neck and head lying flat against the water. This threat, when used by an adult goldeneye toward another duck on the water, is usually convincing. As the belligerent youngster swam toward them, the mallards retreated for a time, then stopped swimming and sat watching the approach of the young duck. Suddenly the mallard hen chopped downward with her bill as she tried to strike the young goldeneye. The terrified warrior turned and ran at great speed over the water to its waiting sibling.

After pairing, many goldeneyes seem to become less tolerant of other ducks on the water about them, even though the pond may be a large one.

May 8, 1976

In the late afternoon when I returned to the cabin from my work in the east forty, life on the pond behind the cabin was in a turmoil. The goldeneye pair was there, but so was an unmated goldeneye drake. I don't know how long this battle had been in progress, but during the time I watched I saw more chasing, more flying from end to end of the pond, more underwater swimming and attacking, then I've seen anywhere this season. As I glassed from the observation deck I could see these males as they swam long distances under water. When the mated drake made his dive, hoping to surface under the unwanted male, the second drake dove also. He swam underwater to some other position on the pond. On one occasion a diving drake surfaced under the unsuspecting, bewildered hen.

Long periods of fighting were followed by short periods of rest. At these times the mated pair swam together, neck to neck. This hen was all around her drake, at times almost on top of him, as she tried to tell him that he was still her man. Ducks, like some humans I've seen in a similar mood, appear to be downright stupid.

May 12, 1976

Three goldeneye hens were involved in a pitched battle on Pond One when I arrived there this afternoon. The picture was confusing for a time, then I realized that a mated female was trying to drive the other hens from this large pond. This feathered fury was quite willing to attack either hen singly or both at the same time. There was chasing on the water, diving and attacking underwater, and pursuit in the air. At one point the mated hen was flying directly over one of the other hens, dropped on the back of the lower bird, carrying her down into the water. When the attacking hen needed a rest she returned to her mate who waited patiently at the other end of the pond. After all, this was a woman's affair; why should he become involved? The intruding hens were still defending their right to stay when I walked away.

Mallards, although larger than feisty goldeneyes, only rarely choose to battle the smaller birds. Mallards are less quarrelsome and generally more tolerant of other ducks on the water with them. But at times they put on a good show.

April 10, 1972

Late this afternoon I saw hard fighting between two mallard drakes on the pond behind the cabin. The mated mallard hen sat quietly on the water, ignoring the fighting going on about her. A short time later, hostilities over, the drakes were swimming about side by side.

May 5, 1977

Two mallard drakes have been swimming together on the pond behind the cabin since noon. When I heard chasing a moment ago, I walked to the deck to see if the mate of one of the boys had arrived. She was there all right, and the friendship was off. The mated drake made it very clear that he wanted the intruder off the water.

Flat-footed Wanderers

May 9, 1977

Two mallard drakes swam in close formation much of the evening. Just two friends with nothing more pressing to do. They ignored, and were ignored by, two goldeneye hens feeding on the pond near them. The lads swam side by side, making precise turns at exactly the same time, robots controlled by the same inner mechanism. When they tired of this game they upended close together as they fed along the shore. I lost interest then and turned back to my book.

When I looked up again the drakes were separated, one with his hen at one end of the pond, the other sitting quietly on the water some distance from the pair. I don't know where the hen came from, I didn't hear her fly in and land. For a time all was quiet on the pond, then the mated drake started moving slowly toward his good friend. When he found himself close enough to the unmated drake to nip him, he did so. Soon there was chasing in the air. Then the lone drake was driven up on shore.

I thought hostilities would end, then, but this was not to be. The aggressive challenger waddled up on shore, drove his old friend back into the water, then resumed the chase. Finally the lone drake flew from the pond. The victor swam back to his hen.

Such intolerance may be just the mood of the moment. In mid-June of 1976 I saw two goldeneye hens asleep side by side on the large log at the pond behind the cabin. A short time later when I heard splashing I walked to the deck and glassed the pond, but saw no ducks. Then, as I watched, a duck broke the surface of the water, struggling wildly and quacking loudly. Suddenly she was thrown free and the second hen surfaced. The plan of battle changed to one of flight

144

and pursuit. Following an interval of quiet when I could see only one duck on the water, the second hen reappeared and the fighting resumed. No drakes and no young involved here—just two disagreeable females shedding their frustrations.

May 6, 1977

Ducks can be almost as unpredictable as some humans I've known. I heard sounds of chasing on the pond behind the cabin. On the water were two pair of goldeneye; two mallard drakes rested on the log on the far shore. One of the goldeneye drakes was trying to drive the other pair from the water. His attacks, which were constant, seemed to be equally divided between drake and hen. His mate fed quietly even though some of the action was taking place near her. There was quiet stalking of the nervous pair, chasing in the air, running on the water, and there were underwater attacks. I left the deck for a short time. When I returned both pair of goldeneye were still on the water. They were now feeding quietly near one another. The mallard drakes were gone.

One may easily wonder as he sees so much violence on the water if jealousy is ever manifested without violence. Is there a hen who doesn't literally wish to tear the feathers out of a trespassing female?

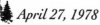

April 27, 1978

For several days I've seen a lone goldeneye hen swimming about with a mated pair. The drake doesn't seem to mind, but his mate has been doing a slow burn. She's driven the single hen away on several occasions. Today as I watched, the drake left his hen and started swimming about with the unmated female. The two had been swimming side by side with bodies touching for only a short time when the mated hen swam in from behind. Gently she forced her body between hen and drake, then swam off with her man. The drake, I noticed, allowed her to do this without protest.

When the fertilization of eggs has been completed and the hen stops laying, the mallard drakes usually join bachelor groups before leaving the area. Goldeneye drakes, in my experience, seem to prefer going it alone for a few days, then they move on. When eggs have hatched and young ducklings are on the water, hens become belligerent and protective of their young. If the drake is still about when the family arrives on the water the hen is quite capable of driving him from the pond.

May 28, 1977

Many times of late I've found a pair of goldeneyes swimming about on Pond One. This seemed unusual, since when the eggs have been fertilized and the hen has stopped laying, the drakes usually head for bachelor country. I was certain that this hen was nesting; other goldeneye drakes have been gone for some time. This morning I found the hen swimming about with eight tiny young in formation behind her. The drake was resting on the water at the other end of the large pond. Why, I wondered, is this hen still tolerating the drake on *her* pond?

Late in the afternoon when I checked again, both hen and drake were still there, one at each end of the pond. Near the goldeneye drake, asleep on downfall, was a mal-

lard drake. The picture was one of peace and content-
ment. Suddenly, with no warning, the hen left the water,
flew to the drake and dropped on him. Although he was
adept at dodging, it did him no good for her attacks were
vicious; she was mad! She chased him in the air, attacked
him underwater, finally drove him to downfall where he
jumped up beside the sleeping mallard. A moment later
the drake jumped back into the water and started swimming as fast as he could, the hen right on his tail. Finally
he took off, circled the pond in the air, and headed east.
I'll probably find him on one of the other ponds in the
morning. The mallard drake was not molested. Contented,
the hen swam back to her family.

The following day I found the banished goldeneye drake
on Pond Eight. His ex-bride seemed to be keeping things
under control on Pond One. Two merganser hens landed
mid-pond; they were attacked immediately. When the mergansers flew to the north end of the pond the challenger
seemed satisfied and returned to her youngsters. When I
arrived back at the pond in the afternoon the goldeneye hen
was just beginning an attack on a ring-necked pair. She
seemed to be directing all of her fury to the ring-necked drake.
Finally he flew from the pond, leaving his mate on the water.
Late in the evening I checked again. The resident goldeneye
and her family had the entire pond to themselves.

 *June 30, 1974*

I had finished mowing the bunkhouse meadow and
was standing at the cabin wondering what to do next when
I heard strange noises from the pond below. I walked to
the observation deck to see what was going on. A golden-

eye hen sat quietly in the middle of the pond; four tiny ducklings ran over the lily pads toward her. It was good to see them on the pond. Then, for a time, the action became confusing. Just as this hen dove and started swimming underwater, I saw a second goldeneye hen at the north end of the pond. Except for short periods of rest, the fighting between the hens was continuous. There was chasing on the water, flying from one end of the pond to the other, underwater attacks. The young ducks seemed to be completely oblivious to any of the action. Finally the intruder left the water, circled the pond in the air, and flew away. Do I detect a slight swagger in the movements of this mother of four?

The next day I was again brought to the observation deck on the run. At first I could see only the four young goldeneyes as they sat quietly on the water. Then a hen surfaced, flapping wings wildly as she pecked viciously at the water. What the hell? As I watched she disappeared under the water again. When she surfaced the next time I saw that there were two hens, both goldeneyes. This girl wasn't pecking at water, she was trying to kill the hen under her! This was a real battle, one with more body contact than any I'd seen all season. The hens swam great distances under water, then resumed their fighting. At one time a hen hid among the reeds at the north end of the pond while the other hen swam on the prowl nearby. I left the deck to turn the horses into the lower meadow. When I returned to the deck the intruding hen was gone. Hens with families on the water seem to have a psychological advantage in these battles.

June 12, 1977

Around four o'clock I walked to the observation deck, watched the young goldeneyes for a time, then sat down to read. I'd been reading only a short time when all hell broke loose on the pond below: wings flapping, ducks quacking, water splashing! The resident goldeneye was at it with a mallard hen. It wasn't until there was a lull in the fighting that I saw that the mallard had arrived on the water with eight young ducklings. When the goldeneye struck again, the young mallards headed for shore. I was certain that some of them would be killed by thrashing adult bodies. What a hell of a way for these young ducks to spend the first few days of their lives.

July 4, 1979

A mallard hen has come with her almost fully grown young to the pond out back where they've been under attack most of the day by the resident goldeneye. While these attacks annoy me, I was amused by the actions of these large young mallards. When they are caught away from shore by the attacking goldeneye and aren't quite sure where the attacker is, they climb up on the lily pads. Although the pad sinks a bit with their weight, the goldeneye isn't able to surface under them. If a human were doing this we would speak of it as intelligence.

When fighting occurs between a goldeneye hen with young and one without a family, the single hen usually leaves. When two hens, each with a family and each determined to remain, start fighting on a pond, there are stormy days ahead.

June 4, 1978

The goldeneye hen who nested in the duck house on the shore of Pond Seven (Family One) moved over to Pond One with her eight-day-old ducklings. The morning after her arrival there the goldeneye hen nesting in a cavity in the snag on the shore of this pond appeared on the water with her family of six (Family Two). Two goldeneye families on the same pond should make things interesting.

This evening I witnessed a pitched battle between the two hens. When I arrived at the pond the two families were widely separated on the water; both families quietly feeding. Very slowly Family One fed toward Family Two. Then, just as I noticed that Hen One was not with her eight-day-old ducklings, she surfaced near Family Two — the battle was on. The larger ducklings hurried to the scene, then just as hurriedly swam away. The tiny ducklings of Family Two, their first day on the water, seemed to pay no attention to the fighting hens. As they continued to feed, they moved slowly toward me.

This fighting was so vicious that for a time I was certain that one, or both, of the hens would be injured. Finally I saw that one of the girls seemed to be winning. Suddenly the hens separated; Hen Two drove her attacker back over the water toward her family. She then flew back to her own end of the pond where she sat quietly on the water. She called softly and six tiny ducklings started swimming slowly toward her. The impatient hen gave a louder command. The youngsters literally fell over one another as they raced toward their mother. For some time then Hen Two thrashed about in the water, making shallow dives, rearranging her feathers. Hen One, the attacker who had not come out so well, sat quietly near her family. It seemed that she'd had enough for now.

I had no way of knowing how many battles between these hens I'd missed, but I did see another intense though short-lived fight late in June. Then, in July, I found these girls in another no-holds-barred contest. There was the usual chasing, one duck riding the tail of the other. At intervals one hen leaped on the back of the other and both went underwater fighting. While they've not settled their own problems, they've accomplished one thing—I no longer worry about either one of them being killed.

Another theater piece, the sex act, is not without its humor for the spectator—although it's probably serious business to the ducks involved.

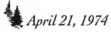

April 21, 1974

I spent much of the day working along the shore of Pond Five, sawing downfall into firewood and burning what couldn't be used in the cabin. For several hours three goldeneye ducks, a drake and two hens, swam together on the pond, seemingly at peace. Then, with no warning that I could see, one of the hens flew at the other and drove her from the drake. Charge after charge was made, yet the drake seemed to pay no attention to the uproar. Finally the aggressive hen made her point. The other hen stayed apart but didn't leave the pond.

For a time the now-mated pair swam about quietly, then to my delight the drake mounted the hen, driving her under water so that only her yellow bill could be seen. Quiet then returned to the pond. Late in the afternoon, the wedded pair left the water for the air and were gone.

In April the following year, I heard fighting on the pond behind the cabin. I grabbed the binoculars and ran to the deck to see three mallard drakes involved in fighting. Somehow, this kind of trouble in the absence of a female seemed odd. Later, when two of the drakes had been driven from the water, a hen I'd not seen appeared. With no preliminaries the remaining drake mounted her, pushing her down so that only her bill and a small portion of her head were visible. If anyone were to ask my opinion I'd say that the hen always seems to be the loser in this game.

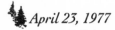

April 23, 1977

White water on the pond behind the cabin brought me on the run with the glasses. For a time the action was so fast that I couldn't tell who was doing the fighting. Then, during a very brief lull, I saw two mallard drakes. There just had to be a hen about somewhere! Several minutes later the ducks separated again just long enough for me to see that the hen was there, right in the center of the fighting. The action had been so fast I'd not been able to count the bodies. For a moment I saw three distinct ducks on the pond, then the unexpected happened. One drake suddenly mounted the hen, then to my surprise, the second drake mounted the drake on the hen. For a time the poor hen was completely submerged. Again they separated briefly, then mounted as before—drake on hen, drake on drake. This happened a third time before the hen was able to escape. She flew to the partially submerged log where she stood indignantly rearranging her feathers. Both drakes swam toward the north end of the pond where one vanished. I assume that he collapsed among the reeds. The other returned to sit beside the hen.

A duck house rests on the shore of each of the four largest potholes on the property. Although I may be relatively certain that a hen is nesting in a house I may never see her either enter or leave it.

May 11, 1977

I try to outwit and outwait a goldeneye hen without success. This female feeds on the pond frequently, and may be nesting in the house on its shore, but no matter how long I wait on the deck, hoping to see her fly to the house, she outwaits me on the pond. Determined to succeed tonight I sat through a long session of feeding, an equally long session of preening and an endless period of just sitting. Finally she took off from the water, circled the pond in the air, and headed toward the house. At the last moment she climbed rapidly and flew out over the tops of the trees.

May 18, 1977

I'm still not certain whether the goldeneye hen is nesting in the house out back. She was here again tonight and I resolved to stay on the deck as long as she was on the pond. She fed, splashed water over her feathers and preened, scratched herself with a foot, and seemed to be making herself at home. Good! When she finally took off from the water I was certain that she was headed for the house. Instead she circled the pond in the air, then made a graceful water landing. We had another wait while she sat arranging her feathers. When she left the water the second time she headed for the house only to circle again and land back on the water. Damn! Another wait during which I became even more eager. It was growing dark;

why the hell didn't she fly to the house while she could still see the doorway? I could barely see her when she left the water for the last time. She circled higher and higher, then to my disgust flew out over the trees.

 *June 10, 1977*

Hooray! I may have been right about the goldeneye hen nesting in the house across the pond. This morning she has six tiny, actively feeding ducklings. They are so small that when they sit on a lily pad, no part of the pad sinks into the water. This afternoon I was amazed to find these young ducks sleeping alone on the partially submerged log across the pond. The hen was nowhere to be seen. Somehow I hadn't expected to see this mother leave her family alone and unprotected on their first day in the water. She was away for about an hour.

I didn't realize until mid-June of 1976 when a goldeneye hen moved her family from Pond One to the pond behind the cabin that these hens travel with their youngsters just as I do in the high country—on foot. Initially when this family appeared on the pond behind the cabin (Pond Three) I thought they had recently hatched here. The hen was placid enough but the young were manic as they dove, ran over the lily pads, and fed. Not until a rest period did I see that they were much too large to be newborn. They stayed on the pond for a few days, then returned to Pond One where they remained until they started to fly.

One year later, again in mid-June, I saw it again. The hen that nested in the house out back threw me a fast one. When I checked the water at nine-thirty in the morning the hen was there with her six young. The entire family was gone at ten. Shortly after ten when I checked Pond Eight I found a goldeneye hen sitting on the water near shore, quacking softly. By ten-thirty this hen had acquired five young. When I glassed the water at eight o'clock in the evening she had a full complement of six. These youngsters were the same size and number as those that left the pond behind the cabin that morning. I can only conclude that this crazy female walked her four-day-old youngsters through high grass, brush, and over or around downfall for one-half mile between ponds. All made the trip safely in five hours or less.

The most restless goldeneye hen in my experience (Family One, 1979) made nine moves with her family of eight in their first nineteen days on the water. The family lived for a time on the pond behind the cabin.

 June 3, 1979

I love these young ducks on the pond out back. When the hen is with them she herds them about, supervising their feeding, their play and their periods of rest. While she was away today the young ducks played. All eight of them dove in unison, then surfaced together. They climbed on, ran over lily pads, then swam in formation. In one of their games seven ducks followed a leader as they swam about with necks and heads flat on the water. They must have been swimming with their eyes closed since the leader collided with a lily pad and was brought to a sudden stop. When the young duck saw what the obstruction was it dove and swam under the pads. Seven siblings then followed their leader under the pads. For me, as I sat typing on the observation deck, this was much like watching a ballet.

When I looked down on the pond the following morning I found the family on their log. The hen stood, stretched, then jumped into the water. One of the youngsters followed immediately. Four others walked down the log into the water, then ran across the water to the hen as she swam toward the center of the pond. The last three ducks waited on the log until their mother was some distance from them, then each made a spectacular jump and a long fast run over the water to the waiting hen.

Then came June 16, 1979, a day of confusion. That morning I had gone to Pond Six with the dogs expecting to find the goldeneyes there. The entire family had been feeding on that pond the night before. But they weren't there, nor was I able to find them on other ponds in the east forty. In mid-morning I found three young ducks of this family asleep on the log across the pond behind the cabin. I was delighted to have these youngsters back again, and to know that the rest of the family would be arriving soon. But when I glassed the water at noon only the hen had been added to the group of three. Five young ducks were still missing. At five, the picture was the same. I was becoming worried; where the hell were the missing ducks?

After the evening meal was finished I checked all ponds in the area thinking that the missing youngsters might somehow have been left behind, hoping to find them alive on one of the other ponds. I found them nowhere. Late in the evening this hen fed with her three youngsters as if the family had never been larger. Although I checked all ponds in the area at least once daily for many days I never saw the missing five again. I think it reasonable to assume that the young ducks were taken by a predator as they walked between ponds. This very restless female never moved the three surviving ducks again. They remained on the pond out back for the next forty-eight days, at which time they were able to fly.

While I had known for some time that many hens lead their tiny ducklings from pond to pond, I'd never actually seen a family on the move. In late May of 1981, I finally met one, but the experience wasn't as pleasant as I had hoped it might be. About nine in the morning I left the cabin with three dogs. We headed south where I planned to begin the day's census of ducks on Pond Eight. The day was bright and warm. The dogs had been trotting quietly beside me when suddenly both Charlie and Frosty swerved to the side. There was a flurry of activity in the tall grass, then Frosty trotted back to me with a dead duckling in his mouth. We had come up behind a hen on the move. Two of the young ducks were killed; I know because I saw them. I can only surmise the fate of the other eight; although I looked for them many times I never saw them again. The hen escaped; I could hear her strident calling from a distant treetop. When we reached Pond Eight she was on the water, still quacking nervously. This old girl had covered half the distance between ponds Five and Eight with her four-day-old ducklings when we came up behind them.

In 1977 I found a lone goldeneye duckling, probably not more than three or four days old, swimming about on Pond Five. This youngster went about the business of feeding and resting as if it didn't know that young ducks of this age were not meant to be alone. I checked on it daily for a period of one month, at which time it disappeared. I have no idea where it came from, nor do I know whether it was taken by a predator or just wandered off.

Two years later I learned that very young ducks will wander overland between ponds without a hen to lead them.

 July 1, 1979

The members of goldeneye Family Four have been separated. When the hen tried to move her ten-day-old ducklings from Pond Five to Pond Eight three of them stopped off at Pond Six A. Three went on to Pond Eight with their mother. This, I think, worries me more than it does either the hen or the abandoned young ducks. I've been wondering if the hen might try to reunite her family. This morning when I found the three young ducks gone from their tiny pond I thought she had probably done so; I thought this until I found the missing three back on Pond Five. They had walked between ponds without a hen to lead them. The goldeneye hen is still on Pond Eight with half of her family.

In two days two of the young ducks disappeared from Pond Five. I suspected that they may have been taken by a predator. I never saw them again. Then, on July 15, two weeks after having been separated from its mother, the last of the young ducks was missing, too. I assumed that it also had been taken by a predator until later the same day when I found the young duck feeding alone on Pond Six. Less than a month old, this duckling had walked from a pond it knew to one it had never seen, without a hen to lead it.

Checking the larger ponds may, at times, be much like watching a three-ring circus. One morning late in May I stood glassing the water of Pond One. My attention span seemed like that of a small child. For a short time I studied the snag on the shore. While I was certain that a bird was nesting in the cavity there, I'd never seen it. A goldeneye pair feeding along the west shore of the pond interested me for a moment. A mallard drake leaving a patch of reeds with two hens took my eye. What was that boy doing with two hens at this time of year? Most mallard drakes have finished their work for the season and have gone from the area. I glassed the snag again before I'd finished checking the water. Damn it, was that female on her nest in the cavity, or wasn't she?

It was at this moment that one of the mallard hens protested loudly, took to the air, then landed again. What the hell had upset her so badly? Next came an explosion on the water to my right, an area that I had not checked as yet. A wildly quacking goldeneye hen shot from the surface of the water in a burst of bubbles. A goldeneye drake rose from these bubbles and flew in pursuit of the hen. Just what goes on here? The hen flew in a graceful arc over the water, then headed directly for the snag. She seemed to fly into the cavity without hesitation at the doorway. I was astonished and delighted; I'm not sure which reaction was the greater. I'd just seen my mystery bird. The drake that had caused it all landed on the water and swam back to his mate. Now I understood it all. The drake left his hen, dove, and swam underwater. He nipped the mallard hen in passing, but his real objective was to drive the other goldeneye hen from the water. I don't suppose that he was as surprised to see the hen enter the cavity as I was.

Even in the world of the duck, there must be some formal instruction of the young. Eight young goldeneye sat on the water facing their mother. Slowly the hen "stood" in the water, her head held high, her body elevated, her tail depressed. She held this position a moment, then forcefully flapped her wings several times before settling back on the water. In unison, then, eight young ducks perfectly imitated their mother. Slowly they too "stood" in the water, flapped their wings vigorously, then settled back on the water again. They had learned their lesson well. School was dismissed, and the family returned to its feeding.

As with the human animal, a mother duck sometimes must raise her voice to get the desired action from her young. With the two dogs I approached a pond on which there was a goldeneye hen with a family of five. Two of the ducklings sat with the hen at the center of the pond; three were on the water near shore. When the dogs walked into the water near the three young ducks, the young ducks were unconcerned. The hen, however, thought differently. A sharp, strident command from her brought the three young ones running.

On occasion I've been able to note the response of hens and their families to loud noises or harassment.

June 14, 1976

I worked near one of the large ponds this morning and happened to be watching a goldeneye family on the water when the quiet was shattered by a mountain-shaking sonic boom. The deafening crash sent the ducks running across the water. Neither hen nor ducklings stopped until they reached the sanctuary of heavy downfall at the end of the pond.

Again in June, one year later, I was just beginning to settle back to my reading after watching a duck fight on the pond below the observation deck when bursts of gunfire, raucous laughter, and catcalls came to us from the west. Obviously Pond One was entertaining visitors. Later, after quiet had been restored, I walked to the pond to learn, if I could, what the hilarity had been about. When I glassed the pond I found the mallard hen on the water with her six young, but I could see none of the goldeneye family. This seemed strange. We started walking along the shore toward the opposite end of the pond. We had covered about half the distance when we flushed seven young goldeneye from their hiding-place in the downfall, near shore. No hen was with them. Not until then did I see the eighth young goldeneye floating belly up near the center of the pond. Those bastards had used the young ducks as targets! Shortly before dusk when I checked again I found that the seven young goldeneye had moved to a narrow, brush-bordered pothole a few hundred yards distant. The hen was not with them.

I have since been able to reconstruct the events of that afternoon. When the revelers appeared at the pond, the mallards, who are shy of people, hid in the brush on shore. Goldeneye ducks, however, seem to pay little attention to anyone moving about on shore. These ducks stayed on the water until they found bullets splashing around them. The hen flew from the pond; at least I did not find her body. The young ducks who were not able to fly raced for shore. Seven made it to the downfall where we found them later; one was killed. Before nine o'clock these young birds had moved to the narrow pothole where the hen had taken them for a brief stay the week before. These young ducks returned to the larger pond a few days later. The hen never rejoined her family.

I have found it difficult to adequately describe the actions of a goldeneye drake or hen when rejoining a mate on the water or giving encouragement to a mate under stress. When pairing in spring, meeting after a brief separation, reassuring one another during a lull in fighting, or gathering after victory, these ducks greet one another with neck and body movements more exaggerated than those used by other ducks in the area. As drake and hen swim to meet one another, their rigidly held necks sway rapidly from side to side. At times the movements are so exaggerated that the duck body sways as well. I learned that this greeting is not reserved only for adults. When a goldeneye hen landed in the pond one day, she clucked softly. As her young ducks swam out from the lily pads the hen greeted them with the usual neck and body wiggles. The young ducks, appearing to synchronize their response, returned the greeting.

On two occasions when I've suddenly come upon a mallard hen with young, the startled hen has reacted with a frenzied and most realistic "injured bird" display.

June 17, 1979

I had finished glassing the tiny pond, had found no ducks on the water, and was walking along a game trail on its shore when something exploded at my side. A mallard hen had been hiding with her family under willow branches that hung over the water. The actions of this agitated female so distracted me that I neither thought to count the youngsters as they raced across the water nor to watch them settle into hiding again. The hen propelled herself forward at great speed, running on the water and using her wings as paddles. Her movement was jerky and erratic. I was fascinated! She ran back and forth, traveled to and fro in an arc, and ran in a circle around and around the tiny pond, quacking all the time as if pursued by the devil. I glassed the pond for some time to see if any of the young ducks would leave their hiding places and rejoin the hen. The hen's complaining did not cease, but it became softer and more natural in tone. None of the young ducks returned to the water while I watched.

Watching ducks on these mountain potholes gives me great pleasure, at times deep peace.

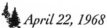

April 22, 1968

For a time this evening I sat with the dogs on the hill across the pond, looking out over the water at the cabin and the Mission Range beyond. I looked into the top of an aspen tree growing on the shore below me. Its leaves were in the delicate lacy stage. On the pond below me two pair of ducks sat quietly on the water. There was no friction between goldeneyes and mallards tonight. I watched the mallard drake when he left the water, circled twice in the air as he gained altitude, then flew away. A short time later he flew in again and made his landing with those beautiful evening-lighted mountains as a backdrop. He seemed to fall straight down with wings spread. The last rays of the sun caught the undersurface of his wings, giving to them a faint reddish hue. There were no sounds other than the duck's soft splashing.

Two months later I discovered a new family on that narrow pothole I call Pond Four. As I dropped to the water's edge I saw six tiny goldeneyes floating in the center of the pond. As I watched these ducklings that could be no more than a day old, they started diving with enthusiasm. When the hen who had been feeding on another pond flew in over the trees and landed, the reunion of mother and young was delightful to see. The young ducks ran about their mother on the water in great excitement. Two, in their glee, climbed on the back of the softly clucking hen, then jumped off into the water again. Finally the hen collected her youngsters on a log lying in the water, climbed up beside them, and all went to sleep.

July 26, 1979

After dinner I wandered to the observation deck where I could see the pond below. Three young goldeneye, all that remain now of the family of eight, were on the water with a mallard family of ten. The mallards are flying now. Suddenly, as if by command, the mallards left the water in formation, flew out over the trees and were gone. It pleased me to have seen this. Not only was the takeoff a pretty sight, but I seemed to enter into the spirit of this new family on the wing.

At the end of July that same year, I had many distractions as I typed on the observation deck. The three young goldeneye were large now. Their afternoon was spent in fun and games. While the third sibling fed quietly, the two more active young ducks dove together, surfaced at the same time, then wildly flapped their wings until they stood in the water. They ran over the water side by side, then ran in arcs, one to the north, the other to the south, until they met again in the center of the pond. Finally the third sibling joined in the fun. The Swan Range, as I saw it from the deck, was free of haze. The sky was cloudless and very blue. Aspen leaves on trees across the water danced in the slight breeze and on occasion hummingbirds flew in to check me on their way to the feeders. Even the horseflies sounded lazy; they were only mildly distracting. The story of these three young goldeneye ended three days later. I wrote, "My three friends spent much of their day yesterday practicing takeoffs and landings. Today they are gone. I shall miss them."

On an afternoon in mid-June a friend and I drove up behind two partially grown goldeneye ducks walking in the road on my property. As neither of us believed that these youngsters could survive the night on land because of predators, we decided to drive them to water. Pond Five lay a short distance to our left; Pond Three lay down the hill to our right. During the next thirty minutes we learned that the driving of young ducks to safety is not the simple task we had pictured it to be. It required great patience, footwork through the timber on game trails, and the hurried planning of each new move.

When, after a long period of frustration, we saw the two ducklings enter the water of Pond Three where they started feeding immediately, both tired herders stood quietly watching through tear-moistened eyes. Somehow one does become emotionally involved with young critters in the wild. By the time I had reached the cabin I found that the young ducks had been joined by a goldeneye hen who must have been on the pond at the time they entered the water. This hen sat before them, talking in great excitement. It took days for me to decide just who these guests might be.

I remembered, then, that on June 11 a goldeneye hen appeared on Pond Six with two newly hatched ducklings. When I checked the pond on June 12, the family was gone. What is more, they disappeared completely, something that goldeneye families rarely do unless the young are taken by a predator. On June 19, the day we found the young ducks walking on the road, I believe that the hen had been leading them toward one of these ponds from a nearby creek. Mallards frequent creeks in this area; goldeneye rarely do. Probably the hen deserted her young when she heard the vehicle coming up over the rise behind her. Possibly she intended to retrieve them when the danger had passed. In our zeal we had inadvertently reunited hen with ducklings. The two young ducks were never moved again; they remained on Pond Three until they were able to fly.

Chapter Eight

NESTERS

I spy on families of birds as some folks watch their neighbors. In 1975 I started building houses suitable for nesting chickadees and nuthatches. That season eight of the thirty-five houses I built were not used. In sixteen of the houses adult birds had been seen carrying food into the house or removing fecal sacs from the nest. Of these sixteen families, fourteen fledged satisfactorily; the two other families of young birds were taken by predators (squirrels) through chewed doorways. Two houses were pulled down by bears; one of these was re-hung and the young birds fledged normally. When all houses were cleaned in the fall, one contained a nest with five unhatched chickadee eggs. Others contained nests of pine squirrels, flying squirrels, or chipmunks.

August 13, 1979

The bird-poop detective! Today I found a three-layered nest in a chickadee house. Earlier in the season I had seen mountain chickadees at that house on several occasions, but had never seen the birds feeding young; I assumed they hadn't remained to nest. But today I found a nest that filled the house to the doorway. The bottom layer, one inch thick, was made entirely of green moss, a filler frequently used by chickadees, squirrels, and chipmunks. The middle layer, less than one-half inch thick, was composed entirely of a fine gray fiber I later identified as shed squirrel hair, which in my experience is used exclusively by chickadees. The upper layer, a thick bed of dry black moss with a deep cup, was fresh and clean. It could have been placed there by squirrel or chipmunk. For a moment I thought the birds had been driven from the house by a squirrel after they had finished building their nest. But when I carefully pulled the nest apart I found bird droppings in the middle layer. There were no unhatched eggs or dead birds, so chickadees had been raised here. The squirrel had built its nest after the young birds left.

A few years later I had more than one hundred houses ready for use by small birds. Each house was given a number and was hung on a trail through the timber. For a few years I walked these trails several times a week, glassing houses and recording what I saw. I learned little information of value in this time-consuming way. I checked one house twenty-five times before I saw birds there feeding young. I glassed another house forty-five times during the season and saw no birds there, yet when I cleaned the house in fall I found a complete chickadee nest heavy with droppings. So my house-rounds became less regular and were eventually discontinued. I gleaned information only when cleaning the houses in the fall.

Although the houses were sturdily constructed, each with a cleanout door, a entryway of proper size, and cavities of recommended dimensions, I soon found that no house was vandal proof. At one house where I had had great satisfaction in watching a nesting red-breasted nuthatch and had seen the adults feeding young, I arrived one morning to find the house deserted, its doorway chewed by a predator—a pine squirrel, I suspect—and the young birds gone. While I was recovering from the disappointment of this loss, I discovered another house with a chewed doorway, a family of young chickadees taken. These houses were in different parts of the property, so two predators had been involved.

After seeing the destruction of the first house I made plans to stud all doorways with metal after the nesting season. But when I found the second family gone, I knew that I shouldn't wait. Studding might not prevent predation, but it should at least slow it down. With a hammer and large tacks I started on my rounds. The first house I walked to was unused, I thought. I drove several tacks in straight, as planned, but sent the next tack in at an angle. Damn! Was the point sticking up in the doorway? I eased my finger into the hole to check. As the tip of my finger disappeared into the cavity, a loud hiss in the house made me pull it out in a hurry. What the hell? It took me more than a moment to gain the courage to try it again. A louder hiss greeted the finger the second time. I finished the studding quickly, then stood back to watch. Several minutes later the head of a chickadee appeared in the doorway. Some time later the bird flew off into the timber. This, I later learned, was an example of "behavioral mimicry." The snake display was very convincing. It is said to be characteristic of both chickadees and titmice.

I walked boldly to the second house, which I also thought

was empty since I had never seen birds there. The studding went smoothly until I became conscious of a calling chickadee near me. I found the distressed bird sitting on a branch above the house. When I stepped back she flew to the house, hesitated on the doorstep, then entered. As I stood before my third "unoccupied" house a head protruded and a chickadee made her exit. I turned to walk away, then heard a pine squirrel scolding in the timber nearby. That squirrel, I decided, was a greater menace than I was. The house was given the full treatment. When I had finished, the bird flew to the house and entered.

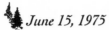 *June 15, 1975*

What a tormentor of nesting birds I've become! On my rounds this morning I found a squirrel near a house that I knew was occupied. Having lost two families to predators I felt that the doorway should be taken care of even though the female refused to leave. The male complained continuously as I worked, his pleading calls coming one after another. When the job was finished the female made her exit. Then both birds started carrying food to their young as if there had been no interruption.

When I tapped on the next house with the hammer no head appeared in the doorway, nor was there a worried bird nearby to plead with me. This operation should be a pleasure, I thought. As I finished studding and started to leave, a chickadee shot from the doorway as if from a cannon. Although this lady quickly disappeared among the trees she had no intentions of making light of her troubles. She continued to call frantically from the timber nearby. After some time her mate appeared. He clung to the doorway, looked in the house, then flew away. If he is looking for his bride, I thought, he should have no trouble finding her. The nonstop complaining of the nervous female continued for some time after her mate left the scene. Finally quiet returned to the forest. The male returned and flew to a limb above the house where he preened. The female fluttered to the house three times and clung to the doorway, but didn't look inside. After a long wait she flew to the house and entered.

That evening when we passed the house the female sat in the doorway watching us with apparent unconcern. She had made an uneventful recovery from the morning's trauma.

I lost no more young birds that year, but the next year all new houses were studded with large, flat-headed roofing nails. Even these did not prove to be predator proof. Eventually I protected all doorways with tin.

During the 1975 season I found two houses pulled from the trees and lying on the ground. The first was a house in which a red-breasted nuthatch had prepared to nest. There was pitch on the house front and a nest in the cavity. She had not as yet laid her eggs. I re-hung the house but it was not used. The second house had been home to chickadees.

June 17, 1975

In mid-afternoon I found a chickadee house on the ground; bear claw marks in the wood told the story. As I stood holding the house, trying to adjust to these happenings in the animal world, I heard two anxious chickadees calling to me from a large serviceberry bush nearby. I quickly re-hung the house, then stepped back to see what the birds would do. Oddly, as soon as the house was back in its proper location, both birds went about the business of feeding themselves and neither went to the house. I stayed about for some time. In the evening I walked back to this house. The studding of the doorway a few days before hadn't driven the birds away, but I wondered if this latest insult might not be too much for the nesting pair. But when the pair flew in both birds carried food into the house. I was amazed! I had known that chickadees were nesting there and had wondered if there might not be eggs in the nest, but these birds were feeding young. I must have arrived shortly after the bear had clawed the house from the tree.

Most chickadees build their nests in May or June. In mid-March of 1976, however, with a subzero temperature and a snow cover that was almost complete, I found a pair of chickadees whose thoughts seemed to be only of love and little ones. To my surprise one of the excited birds carried twenty-three loads of dark moss into the house during the short time I watched. I saw no activity about this house during the rest of the season but in the fall I found the nest heavy with droppings.

The red-breasted nuthatch is an intense little bird. In the days of reasonable prices I kept a feeder filled with doughnuts well into the summer months. I recall a day when a red-breasted nuthatch appeared with her family of young. The feeder was empty at the time and the bird had nothing but crumbs to feed the youngsters. She waited impatiently as I walked toward the feeder with a doughnut. She became even more excited as I placed the food in the feeder. She talked continuously as she carried large chunks of food to her ravenous family. My closeness did not bother her in any way.

One day in early May, as I glassed a house in the east forty, I saw that black moss had been caught in fresh pitch about the doorway. The coating of pitch was so thick that some of it had run down the front of the house. When I tapped on the house a red-breasted nuthatch appeared in the doorway, stared at me for a moment, then dropped out of sight again. I was puzzled; what was the purpose of the pitch? Later, when checking the reference books in my library, I found a discussion of pitch and the red-breasted nuthatch in only one of them. The nuthatch, it seems, collects pitch from trees in the area and places it about the doorway of the cavity in which it is nesting. No other bird does this. No one has a satisfactory explanation for this odd behavior.

Later in the month a pair of nuthatches took over a new house near the cabin.

 May 26, 1975

Late in the afternoon as I walked toward the cabin I heard the raucous call of a red-breasted nuthatch. When the pair flew in they went directly to the new lodgepole house hanging near the cabin. The excited birds examined the house, each bird inspecting the inside, outside, and roof. Both birds then flew to a nearby fir tree, pecked at its branches, and returned to the house where they left tiny balls of pitch on the doorway. Each bird made about fifteen such trips, rarely returning to the same tree two times in succession. Their excitement indicated to me that they had only recently discovered the birdhouse. Perhaps they were indicating by the pitch that they had chosen to nest there. No nesting material was carried into the house at the time of this first visit.

🌲*June 11, 1975*

On several occasions the male nuthatch has flown in and placed pitch around the doorway. Today I saw him fly from a fir tree to the house where he placed his offering of pitch. While he was still in position near the doorway the female arrived, pushed him aside, and entered the house. She is either laying or brooding eggs. This male usually appears early in the morning and again in the evening. He flies in silently, clings to the doorway and twitters softly, as if alerting the nesting female that he is there. This done, he places his load of pitch either about the doorway or on the front of the house, then flies away. Even after the eggs were hatched and both parents were busily feeding their offspring, the occasional bead of pitch was added to the house-front. I'm not certain what day the youngsters fledged, yet when I realized that they had gone, I knew I had sustained a loss. They had become part of my family.

🌲*April 3, 1976*

I stopped and listened, then traced the tapping to an old fir snag where a red-breasted nuthatch was preparing a nesting cavity. A doorway of the proper size had already been formed; the bird was now starting work on the cavity itself. One of my birdhouses hung on a tree trunk not far from the snag. Either this pair had not seen it, or they preferred their own materials and design.

Initially both birds worked on the cavity, one flying off when relieved by the other. But after a few days of shared labor the female took full responsibility. The male, noticeably larger with a more brightly colored breast, escorted the lady to work in the morning then flew off when she entered the cavity. Two times when she knew he was outside, his bride left the cavity as if inviting him to take over; when he didn't, she went back to work again. Occasionally the pair flew off together to feed. I checked on the progress being made from one to three times daily. Usually I sat on a log on the forest floor far enough away to watch in comfort. I could hear tapping when the bird was working. When she came to the doorway to dump her load, I could see powder and tiny chips float slowly to the ground. On two occasions I saw the weary female leave the cavity and cling to the side of the snag where she seemed to doze. She was soon back in the cavity working again.

May 2, 1976

Today the action changed. When I arrived at the snag this morning I saw neither nuthatch about. A sapsucker flew in, landed on the snag, and explored its surface. The bird had finished a thorough inspection of the nuthatch cavity and had moved to another part of the snag when the male nuthatch arrived. Wow! The action was fast! This tiny bird drove the sapsucker from tree to tree, then from the area. When the large bird was gone the nuthatch returned to the snag where he thoroughly checked the cavity. Then he flew away.

May 12, 1976

I arrived at the snag this morning in time to see the male nuthatch tangle with a sapsucker for the second time. Today, the larger bird flew from the snag to a nearby tree where it indicated, at least to me, that it planned to remain. The little warrior charged again and again, pecking fiercely at the larger bird. Finally, when the sapsucker did fly off, the feisty nuthatch flew to its perch.

By May 29 the layer of pitch glistening about the doorway was so thick that I could see it from the ground without
the use of binoculars. Then, early in June, I watched like a
happy grandfather as the female flew from the cavity with a
fecal sac. Both birds were now busily feeding young. What a
delightful series of observations I would have missed had
these birds chosen to nest in one of my houses.

No status is gained by seeing a robin, unless it is the first
robin to arrive in spring. For a while each spring these birds
hang in the meadow in flocks, then suddenly one sees only
the occasional pair. The birds have started nesting.

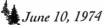

June 10, 1974

A robin has been trying to build her nest on a projecting log at the horse barn. The space in which she is working is markedly limited by the overhanging roof. As I
watched this morning, each time the lady flew to the nest
site with building material, her mate followed and tried
to mount her in this cramped space. Since this was physically not possible, the female was routinely forced to the
ground, still carrying the bedding. There she was duly
mounted by the male. I watched as this act was replayed
four times, then decided that the amorous male was the
lady's problem, not mine. I walked into the barn to saddle
Piccolo. When I returned from my ride the girl was sitting in the finished nest. Tonight the nest contains one
egg.

For several years I did mirror examinations on all the
robin nests. I counted eggs as they appeared, noted lengths
of incubation periods, and watched young birds as they grew.
In doing this I earned the undying hatred of a nesting fe-

male. One day I climbed to her nest thinking she was away feeding—she wasn't. After that slight error the female dived at me whenever, or wherever, I appeared in the yard. She could neither forget nor forgive.

When there are young birds in the nest and the mirror appears above them, those big mouths with their bright yellow lining open, waiting to be filled. Fecal sacs, which are usually expelled when the young bird is fed, are either eaten by the adult or carried some distance from the nest.

On a bright afternoon in midsummer when a nest is flooded with sunlight, being a proper parent presents added problems. On several occasions I've seen a robin whose nest was built on a west-facing log of the cabin as she protected her babies from the heat of the sun. The bird stood on the rim of the nest, its wings elevated so that the young birds were shaded. The neck of the adult was extended upward so that her head was shaded by the overhanging roof. Her mouth was open and she was panting.

June 22, 1975

As the sun peeped over the mountain this morning, I walked near the robin's nest on my way to the barn. Two young robins were in the nest; a third youngster stood on the rim. The adults fussed as they flew from tree to tree. When I walked back to the cabin after feeding the horses the nest was empty and the young birds had been spirited away. I understand, now, what took place in that nest just before dusk last night. The picture in the nest was much the same as it was this morning—two birds in the nest and one standing on the rim. An adult flew from the barn roof, landed on the rim knocking the young bird back into the nest. Then, with its neck and head the adult forced all three youngsters to lie down. Dusk, it would seem, is not the proper time to have young birds on the loose for the first time.

Only rarely have I been directly involved in the fledging of young robins. However, the two times I was involved, I proved to be the loser.

June 15, 1967

After giving the horses their evening pellets I looked in on the young robins in the meadow shed. They were large and I thought should be leaving soon — little did I realize how soon. It was a beautiful evening! I climbed the fence near the shed, sat on the top rail and looked at the mountains. Both Penny and Waif were sniffing about below me. This idyllic interlude ended abruptly when Penny barked and I heard the scolding of robins. Damn! At the shed I found chaos. Three young robins hopped aimlessly about on the ground; the fourth was in the mouth of my elkhound. The old folks were frantic. I bellowed and Penny dropped the unharmed bird.

It was at this point that I made my first mistake. I reasoned that if the young robins had been frightened from the nest by the barking of a dog, they should be returned to the nest. I had no trouble in catching the first bird. When I had placed it in the nest I left in pursuit of a second. This wasn't proving to be such a problem, after all. However, when I carried the second bird to the nest, the first bird was no longer there. Obviously this wasn't going to work.

I climbed the fence at some distance from the shed, then watched through the binoculars to see if adult rob-

ins had a better way of handling things. A parent carrying a worm in its bill hopped into the shed. A moment
later it appeared again, followed by a young robin. When
the young bird hesitated, as it frequently did, the parent
pretended to offer the worm. Then, as the young bird
started moving and reached out for the worm, the adult
hopped on. When parent and child reached the fence,
the parent hopped to the lower rail. As soon as the youngster sat on the lower rail, the adult moved to the upper.
The young robin was given the worm when it sat on the
upper rail.

Now I made my second error. I reasoned that the adults
probably wanted all of their children to spend the night
on the rail fence. I knew that one of the young birds was
"lost" in the high grass near me. Perhaps I should lend a
hand. As my hand moved toward the hidden bird, its
mouth opened probably thinking it was going to be fed.
But, when my hand closed about its body the uproar began. The youngster struggled and screamed for help; the
adults flew at my head. Chastened by the attack of the
adults I dropped the young bird and climbed back on the
fence. To hell with the lot of them! The child quickly forgot its fear and went back to sleep in the tall grass. Quiet
gradually returned to the meadow. A short time later I
saw one of the adults following a fluttering young bird.
The child was leading, not the adult. Why these parents
wanted one child on the rail and didn't much care where
the others slept, I couldn't say.

 *July 27, 1968*

After I finished washing the windows, this morning, I
sat on the railing in the sunlight. I glanced into the hole in
which my new twelve-hundred gallon cistern now rests.

That concrete tank should be buried soon. I felt relaxed and very pleased with my life. Slowly some unusual crackling sounds wormed their way into my dreams; sounds which seemed to be coming to me from the hole below. I walked to the edge and looked down. There a young robin was walking about on newspapers I had used in wiping the windows.

I climbed down to rescue the youngster. As I moved slowly toward the bird it fluttered into a narrow space between the dirt wall and one end of the concrete tank. Damn! I climbed out of the hole to plan my next move. After driving the bird out into the wider portion of the cavity by dangling a broom from above, I placed strips of waste plywood across the narrow opening, then climbed back into the hole. Again, the bird fluttered into the same narrow space. The plywood hadn't completely closed the opening. For the second time I climbed out, dangled the broom from above, rearranged the strips, then dropped back into the cavity. The uncooperative brat still led me a merry chase. Finally my hand closed about the bird and I tossed it to the surface. I had won; another life saved. The adults were still raising hell with me as I walked away.

Mountain bluebirds mean beauty, sweetness, gentleness, innocence—any of these words seem to fit. Yet I have seen these gentle birds chew the pants off trespassing tree swallows when defending their nests. For several years after my arrival in the valley the only houses available to bluebirds were hung on the south-facing wall of my old log barn. All three of these houses had doorways that were much too large, but I didn't know that at the time.

After a few seasons of observing these birds I learned that there seems to be a definite pattern to bluebird nesting behavior. Initially both birds inspect the houses with enthusiasm. Then for a time the interest of the female seems to wane. This little lady sits demurely on the rail fence and doesn't go near a house. During this period the male displays even more enthusiasm. He sings from the barn roof, he sings from the roofs of the houses, he enters each house and sings from its doorway, and he sings to his mate as he sits beside her on the fence. At this stage both birds may leave the property, at which time the landlord worries that the birds may find more desirable accommodations elsewhere. If they return, and they usually do, the female starts gathering material for her nest at once. As she works the male sings to her and gets in her way. When the lady starts sitting on eggs the male is not much in evidence, but when it is time for the eggs to hatch he returns to haunt the place. When the male clings to the doorway as he looks into the house, one may feel reasonably certain that there are young birds in the nest. Both parents will soon be feeding young.

I didn't know all of this when I first hosted a bluebird pair in 1966.

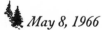 *May 8, 1966*

Mountain bluebirds have been inspecting the houses on the south wall of the old barn. Until today greater interest in this business has been shown by the colorful male. He has spent much of his time entering the houses, sitting in their doorways, or singing to the female as she sits on a house roof. But today this girl has decided that raising a family may have its rewards. She is building her nest. Unfortunately she doesn't seem to know which of the houses she prefers, and is carrying nesting material into each of the three houses. She has been working steadily now for an hour. As she hops about gathering grass, the male sings to her from a house roof. When she enters a house with her load, he flies to the doorway, looks in, and blocks her exit. The hard-working female must push him aside if she wants to get on with her work.

Somehow this building of nests in three houses has been bothering me. I picture all manner of complications resulting from such indecision. So, during the temporary absence of the pair this morning I blocked two of the doorways with brown cloth, then stepped back to see what would happen. As I might have expected, I suppose, when she returned to work the female tried to carry her first load into a house with a blocked doorway. What a frustrated girl she was! She flew to the roof of the barn, then dropped to the house and again tried to enter. Finally she placed her load of grass into the one house with an open doorway; then both birds flew away.

At this point I was ready to admit to a monumental blunder. Up went the ladder again. I unblocked the doorways, then went about my other chores. The pair returned later in the day and the female resumed the building of all three nests.

This female who seemed so indecisive in choosing a house in which to nest managed nicely without further help from me. On June 11 the pair began feeding young.

The following year bluebirds again chose to nest in one of the houses on the old barn. This time the female built in only one of the houses. Again the male was more enthusiastic than helpful. One morning when the female flew to the house with nesting material she found her man sitting in the doorway looking out. As he made no move to leave, she flew to the roof of the barn and waited. Three times she dropped to the house with bedding; each time she found her mate blocking the entrance. On several occasions, too, when the female carried nesting material into the house, the curious male clung to the doorway blocking her exit.

One morning when nest-building was still in progress I saw this male sitting in the doorway holding a large white feather in his bill. The female saw him there too and flew to the roof of the barn with her load of grass. Nothing was being accomplished. After what seemed like a long period of waiting she flew to the house, forced her way inside, dropped her load and made her exit. A moment later the male again appeared at the doorway, still carrying his feather. Where he eventually took his treasure I don't know. I last saw him sitting on the barn roof still holding the feather in his bill. I do know, though, that when the time came to feed his family, this boy worked as hard as his mate.

In 1968 the female member of the bluebird pair seemed to be the more feisty family member. It was she who took on the swallows when they trespassed. Although she had not yet started building, she gave every indication that she intended to stay. The swallows were unusually troublesome that year. After several days of challenge I noticed a sudden change in the thinking of this tough little girl. She sat calmly on the meadow fence, ignoring tree swallows as they moved in and out of her houses. The male bluebird then took up the fight unaided by his mate. On two occasions I saw him fighting swallows, always two swallows to one bluebird, yet the female didn't stir from her chosen place on the fence. Late in the afternoon, that day, the bluebirds flew off. I didn't see them again until they returned to the meadow with their young in tow. The swallows, once they had rid the place of bluebirds, didn't stay to nest, either.

The following year we started the season with new blue-bird-swallow houses in the meadow. The bluebirds moved from the houses on the old barn to a new house in the lower meadow; better for the bluebirds but less satisfying for me. For several years after that I hosted a pair in the lower meadow. In 1975 the pair nesting in the south meadow provided me with the greatest interest. There the female built her nest in the usual manner, laying and brooding her eggs. On several occasions during brooding I saw the male fly to the house carrying a caterpillar in his bill. Each time he entered the house with the offering of food and came out without it. He was feeding his mate. When young birds appeared both male and female busily carried food into the house. My notes of that year show that the female was last seen about the house on June 19. After that date only the male was seen feeding young—and a very busy chap he was.

June 27, 1975

When I checked the house in the south meadow this evening I found it empty. As always my reaction was one of happiness for the family even though I knew there would be an empty spot in my daily routine. I removed the nest, closed the clean-out door, and moved on. I hadn't gone far when I heard the excited calling of young blue-birds. With the dogs following me I moved slowly through the young timber toward the excited youngsters. At first I saw only one young bird sitting on the top rail of the meadow fence. I heard other voices but couldn't see birds.

Before long the adult male had herded the other two young birds to the fence. Then he started to carry food to them. This boy seemed to thoroughly enjoy his responsibilities as he fed his young family. One can only speculate as to what might have happened to the female; except for the first two days of feeding, these young birds were raised entirely by the male.

In 1978 my bluebirds kept me guessing. By the time I had decided that I actually did have two pair nesting on my property, I found a third pair who were obviously looking for accommodations. I saw this pair first in an old sawmill site near the south border of the property. The female was building her nest in a cavity in an ancient snag. I was elated! Then, as I watched, a flicker flew in and took possession of the snag. Damn! I wanted that third pair of bluebirds. I hurried back to the cabin for a new house, which I hung where I was certain the bluebirds would see it. They saw it, all right, but ignored it. That house was soon taken over by swallows. I rushed back to the cabin for a second house, which the bluebirds showed no interest in either. When they passed up a third house I had hung especially for them I decided that I couldn't tell from their actions just what type of accommodations they wanted. It was obvious that they were not looking for a custom-built birdhouse. Finally this pair found a satisfactory cavity in an old snag, nested, and raised four young.

The other two pair didn't do as well that year. Of five young bluebirds in the house in the lower meadow, only three fledged. I found two dead birds in this house. Of the three living youngsters I had seen in the house in the south meadow, two died in the nest. Food was scarce because of dryness, so some of the young birds starved. Undaunted by the problems of the first nesting, the bluebirds in the lower meadow decided to nest a second time.

July 1, 1978

While the female busies herself about her second nesting, this time in a house near the horse barn, her colorful mate has taken on the chore of feeding the three young of their first family. Both birds seem to enjoy what they are doing. At times the male fed his youngsters near the bunkhouse where I worked on a new fence. He seemed to delight in his responsibilities, since he sang as he fed his young.

Gradually these young birds have started feeding on their own. Yesterday only one young bird flew in with the male. This morning he was alone in the meadow. Tonight one of the young birds was with him again. Father and child started feeding at opposite ends of the fence between meadows. As it fed, the young bird slowly moved toward the adult male. Suddenly the adult charged. He drove the young bird from the fence to a ponderosa nearby. I was as startled by the suddenness of this attack as the youngster must have been. The male continued the assault as he drove this bird from limb to limb. When the young bird flew from the meadow, the adult flew in pursuit. The family bond is broken. There was no mistaking the intentions of this adult male. He was protecting his territory—reserving it for his second family.

The barn swallows using the loft of the old barn for their nursery seemed destined for trouble. The first nesting of this pair was a total failure. Four young birds lay dead on the floor below the nest. After a period of rest the pair decided to try again.

August 13, 1966

Today another catastrophe! When I walked out of the cabin after lunch I saw the swallow pair flying in and out of the loft in great excitement. The distraught birds called continuously. I climbed to the loft to see what had happened. Two very young birds were still in the nest, which lay on the floor, and a third bird lay on the floor nearby. Judging by the actions of the adults the nest must have just fallen. I looked about, saw one of my hanging horseshoe feeders, placed the nest in the feeder, the birds in the nest, and hung the feeder from the ridgepole. Although the nest is now a bit lower than it was and will swing freely when a bird lands or takes off, at least it is off the floor. But will the adults use it?

Even though the pair continued to fly in and out of the loft, I had no proof that they had accepted the freely swinging nest. The loft was so dark that I couldn't see the nest when standing on the ground in the sunlight. Finally, on the third day, I took the feeder down just long enough to be certain that at least two of the young birds were alive and growing. Then ten days after the catastrophe, excited swallows again flew about in the space between the cabin and the old barn. This time, though, the mood of the birds seemed different. In the loft the hanging nest was empty; all three of the young birds had fledged. This, I might add, was the origin of my unique, freely swinging, swallows' nest that has been rebuilt and reused many times during the ensuing years.

Over the years I have watched barn swallows build nests, both birds actively working until the nest was ready for occupancy. Using a mirror I've counted the eggs as they appeared, usually one egg each day, and I've watched the females care for them. When I checked a nest in the horse barn on one July evening as I waited for the horses to finish their pellets, all five eggs were neatly standing on end. The female flew in, busied herself about the nest, then flew out again. All five eggs had been turned on their sides.

I've seen adult birds standing at each end of the nest, looking down at the newly hatched young. If they had been humans watching their baby in the crib we might have said that they were expressing pride and love. Newly hatched youngsters must be protected from chill. I stood in Piccolo's stall one evening when the female swallow prepared to leave her nest. She stood on the rim shaking and separating soft white feathers with her bill, much as one might shake rugs or bedding. All young birds were covered with a layer of feathers before she flew from the barn to feed on the wing.

I hadn't known, but soon learned that when the birds are very young the fecal sacs are removed from the nest by an adult. But when the young are larger and stronger, they turn in the nest and poop over the rim on whoever, or whatever, is below. The first time I saw an almost fully grown youngster clinging to the side of the nest and wildly flapping its wings I thought the bird had slipped while relieving itself. I was quite certain that it had caught the nest as it fell and was struggling to climb back in. Not until I saw two birds doing this at the same time did it occur to me that they might be exercising their wings in preparation for the day of fledging.

Dry years, when bugs are scarce, take their toll on swallows. On a day in August when I checked the young barn swallows in the horse barn I found the four birds sleeping quietly. Everything appeared to be normal. Two days later when I walked into the barn I saw that the wing of one bird hung awkwardly over the side of the nest. Four very dead birds now lay in the nest. Starvation had taken its toll.

In July of 1978 when I walked to the barn to pellet the horses I found the sky filled with swallows. The nest was empty, but one young bird had dropped only to the rail of the stall below. There it sat, showing no concern when I passed only a few feet from it. I stood in a dark corner of the barn watching the adults as they tried to entice this last young bird out of the barn. For some time the youngster refused to believe that flying could be more fun than sitting. Time after time both adults flew into the barn, dipped and turned before the young bird, then flew out again. The young bird ignored them. Finally, as the pair continued to perform for their child, it started to "dance" with excitement; then it took to the wing and flew out behind its parents. It flew well.

As the families of barn swallows progress from the egg stage toward the fully fledged, some of the old folks became irascible and overprotective of their home territory.

June 29, 1973

When they first appeared this year the swallows nesting in the horse barn showed great tolerance toward their landlord. During periods of courting, nest building and laying I was allowed to enter and leave the barn without fanfare. But after the hatching of the eggs my presence became an irritant, and as the young increased in size the

pair became even more paranoiac. As the time for fledging neared, these adults met me in mid-meadow; they
harassed me continuously until I entered the building.
These scolding, diving birds both amused and annoyed
me as they flew at me, turning only at the last moment to
avoid hitting me.

On the day the young birds left the nest I was able to
repay with kindness the attacks these temperamental elders
had made upon me. Whether this kindness will make con-
verts of the old sinners I shall probably never know. As I led
Piccolo to the barn after my ride today I found a young swallow floating in the stock tank. Although thoroughly drenched,
the bird was still alive; the accident must have happened
shortly before my arrival. The irascible parents watched as I
picked the young bird out of the water. They showed no
hostility as I stood holding their child, wondering what should
be done. I placed the youngster on the rail fence, thinking it
would dry quickly in the sunshine. A moment later it toppled
and fell to the ground. I carried it to the picnic table near the
bunkhouse. The adults sat on the fence watching me. For a
time the young bird sat quietly, its feathers drying in the
sunlight. Suddenly it rolled and lay with its feet in the air.
Damn, this wouldn't do! I made a nest of grass on the table
top, then transferred the youngster to the nest. As its feathers dried the bird began to exercise its wings. After a long
period of drying the young bird took to the air, gliding as
much as flying in an arc around the corner of the bunkhouse.
Somehow I had the feeling that this young swallow couldn't
fly where it wanted to go. Probably because of this defect it
landed in the tank in the first place.

Nesters

🌲 *July 6, 1973*

No adult swallows dove at me as I walked to the horse barn this morning, even though their family was sitting on the fence nearby. I couldn't be certain that the fifth youngster was with them as there was too much activity for an accurate count.

🌲 *July 8, 1973*

I was late in giving the horses their pellets tonight and when I stepped into the barn I found the young swallows already asleep on their perch just inside the door. When they flew from the barn one of the young birds, probably the one I found in the water, hit the door casing and fell to the ground. As I stood there looking down at the grounded swallow the adults gave me everything they had, scolding as they dove directly at me. The young bird made two unsuccessful attempts to fly. With its third try it became airborne and flew off with its parents.

The next day when I returned from my ride I found five young barn swallows sitting on the fence waiting to be fed. All seemed to be doing well. Later in the day the sky near the cabin seemed to be filled with flying, gliding, soaring, and dipping swallows. Both families, those from the horse barn and those from the loft, were involved in this aerial ballet. Early in the evening two little swallows sat resting side by side on the rail fence. The pace had been a little too strenuous for them to maintain.

Sometime during the first warm days of March or April a distant thumping sound is carried as gracefully as swallows on the soft, warm air. The sound is slow and deliberate at the start, then it accelerates until it ends in a muffled roar. This is the wing-beating challenge of the polygamous male ruffed grouse to another male grouse. It is also an invitation to any receptive female of his own kind. The sound fills the season when one may happen upon a nesting female grouse, always a surprise.

Found in timbered areas, grouse nests are not remarkable. The hen scrapes a slight hollow in the ground at the base of a tree, stump, rock, log, or bush. The hollow may be carelessly lined by leaves, conifer needles, and matted feathers. When the hen is surprised on the nest she "explodes" from the ground at one's feet, gives a raucous squeal or whine, and promptly goes into a crippled bird display that she hopes will lead the intruder away from the nest.

 *June 16, 1971*

In the evening as I walked in the east forty, murmuring softly to myself, I startled two does lying in the brush. Both bounded away. A short time later a ruffed grouse burst from the brush at the side of the trail with such strident moaning that I jumped backward. I watched with fascination as she demonstrated an almost-believable injured bird display. Not only did this girl demonstrate a broken wing on the right, but an injured left wing as well. She rotated her injuries from side to side, moving in an arc as she dragged the injured wing. This pitiful picture was accompanied by most realistic cries of pain and fear. Before I had fully adjusted to the situation the elkhound lunged at the bird. Her recovery was instantaneous, but once safe from the dog she resumed her demonstrations. I could still hear the raucous moaning of the hen when we were well down the trail, out of her sight.

Four years later, again in the middle of June, another grouse shot off her nest and limped away as I watched. Again the loud wailing was a prominent part of her display. I followed her for a time, then walked back to the nest. Five eggs lay on the ground surrounded by a ring of leaves and pine needles. A sixth egg had rolled some distance from the nest. The next day I found the nest vandalized and the hen gone. Two eggs in the nest were unbroken, one egg was cracked, and there were shell fragments scattered over much of the area.

In 1979, again in mid-June, after checking a large pond in the southern part of the property, the dogs and I headed back toward the cabin on a game trail. Suddenly Charlie, who was leading, lunged into the timber and sent a ruffed grouse off on her display. This hen compensated for her less-than-perfect acting by the intensity of her wailing. I watched her a moment, then found her nest at the base of a lodgepole pine. She had been sitting on nine eggs; one of which had rolled from the nest during her hasty departure. I placed this egg back in the nest and we walked on. Two days later, with both dogs under control behind me, I walked slowly toward the tree, then stopped to glass the ground at its base. I was confused; I couldn't see the nest, yet I felt certain that I was checking the right tree. As I raised the glasses for a second look the hen moved her head and I caught a momentary reflection of light from one eye. The color of the nesting bird matched the color of the lodgepole bark so perfectly that she had been well hidden. We backed away without disturbing her.

The following night I found this nest deserted, the hen gone, and all the eggs broken. I was depressed! But as I walked back toward the cabin I began to wonder what predator could so neatly split all eggs in halves without cracking the half-shells. I thumbed through texts in my library until I found a picture of an identical nest. These young birds had hatched normally. They were off in the forest with their mother.

I recall one grouse hen who might easily have been the product of a finishing school. Instead of being a raucous exhibitionist, as were other members of the family, this demure little girl was silent. As I was walking through the forest with the dogs, one day, I saw her silently leave her nest when we were still some distance away. Instead of the usual, carelessly built nest, hers was meticulously constructed with thick walls of down, two inches high. In the nest nine eggs lay neatly on their sides on a thin layer of down.

On my next visit the hen was out feeding; the eggs were covered with a thick layer of down, and the nest was difficult to find. I checked this nest at two-day intervals. I was becoming more anxious as the time for hatching neared. Then came a day of shock when I arrived to find the eggs destroyed and the hen gone. Shell fragments were strewn about a wide area. On two previous visits I had heard a noisy raven family near the pond below. Now I found a large splash of "whitewash" on the ground a few feet from the nest; another on a bush nearby. The ravens had gorged on grouse eggs.

It is said that ruffed grouse can be both fearless and aggressive. I became a convert to this belief after meeting with a hen in June of 1979. I had been checking ponds in the east-forty and was walking back to the cabin on a game trail. The hen exploded underfoot and at the same time I saw young grouse of some size flying into an area of brush. This hen displayed in such a raucous, realistic way that even the two dogs sat quietly behind me, fascinated by her acrobatics. She traveled in an arc, only a few feet at a time, using only one wing and dragging the other. None of us moved. After she had traveled for some distance, she turned and worked her soundless way back toward us. Then she was off on another deafening display. The young birds, of course, were all well hidden. Suddenly this hen shot from the ground and flew directly at my face, swerving only at the last minute to avoid hitting me.

I met one hen whose genteel display had me completely confused for a time. Initially I could see only the odd movements of her head and the shaking of the low brush which hid her body. These movements were accompanied by soft, strangling sounds. I wondered if she was being attacked by some predator that I couldn't see. But as the hen moved slowly out from behind her cover I saw that she was beating the ground with partially folded wings. This was the explanation for the unusual movements of her head, and the shaking of the brush. As she moved slowly off into the forest I realized that she must have been with young birds, and that she was giving them a chance to scatter and hide. Possibly if we had continued to move toward her she would have gone into a classic injured bird display. We waited quietly. She walked slowly, barely limping as she moved toward a fallen tree. There she jumped easily up on the trunk. She continued her soft moaning until we were well on down the trail.

For a few moments, then, there was silence, after which she started to cluck softly. The danger was over; the hen was calling her scattered chicks.

Even the most casual observer of nesting birds must, I suppose, have moments of triumph. I have had two, the first a baby owl, the second a family of merlins. In June of 1978, a baby owl had fallen from a nest cavity high in a rotten snag. It was sitting on the forest floor when it was seen by a friend walking her dogs. As there was no chance of returning it to the cavity in the snag, and since we doubted it could survive the night on the ground, the baby came home with me. It was a beautiful bird with a body clothed in feathers of light gray, flecked with brown. Its eyes were brown; both feet and its bill seemed many sizes too large for its body. Not until I had reached the cabin did I begin to wonder what care the bird should have—what would it eat, and how often should it be fed? I decided to check the little owl every two hours during the night. At midnight my new friend was voracious, eating hamburger from the palm of my hand. But at two it showed little interest in food. It would swallow only if the food was put in its mouth. At four the baby refused all food, and when I tried again at seven only tiny bits of meat were taken. By this time I was certain that the little guy was dying! However as the day progressed, the youngster became more alert. I began to wonder, then, if its lack of interest in food might not have been caused by the fact that it wasn't hungry and wanted to sleep.

My friends, the Berners, took the owl the next night. The following morning I put an alert little owl on the desk of Dr. Phil Wright at the University of Montana in Missoula. Phil said that he had found just the person to raise it.

Late in June I learned that the baby was growing rapidly and that it could jump to great heights in its flying cage, but wasn't ready to fledge. I was amused to learn that the owl "kills" each frozen mouse it is offered before eating it.

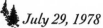 *July 29, 1978*

Today Chris Servheen and his wife Cindy, the couple who raised the young owl, appeared with the grown bird. It is now a large and handsome barred owl. Chris tells me that this is the first authenticated nesting of a barred owl in western Montana. When the bird was released across the pond behind the cabin it flew first to an ancient stump, then dropped to the ground where it remained until flushed by Chris. It flew, then, to successive perches, each new perch a little higher than the last one. About nine tonight the bird was still in the area where it had been released. When it saw me it bowed and talked as it had done when released. It showed no interest in the mouse I offered, but watched as I laid it on a nearby stump.

July 31, 1978

On morning and evening checks at the release point I've not seen the owl, nor has the mouse been taken. To-night, for the first time, the mouse was gone. A western tanager and several small birds were scolding as I walked out to the road. There, across the grassy triangle at the Y, sat the owl. Obviously it was a worry to the smaller birds. The bird watched me until I began moving slowly toward it. Then it turned, took to the air, and with slow, powerful wing beats disappeared around a bend in the road. Gradually the small birds stopped fussing, and quiet returned to the area. The mouse I placed on the stump that night was never taken, nor did I see the owl again. But since that evening, whenever I hear the call of a barred owl, I like to think that it is the chap who spent a troubled night in my cabin.

I glassed the cavity in that large snag every time I checked the pond's surface for ducks, trying to determine what, if any, nesting bird was in residence. Over a period of several summers these observations had been futile; I had never seen a bird either enter or leave the cavity. Then early one morning in the middle of May I sensed, rather than saw, that something in the cavity was blocking the entrance. After a long wait a head was thrust through the opening, a head wearing a golden crown in the direct morning sunlight. A few minutes later the bird made its exit. This bird was jay-sized and golden-brown in color; she flew low over the trees with steady wing beats. I had no idea what the bird might be. Back at the cabin the bird guides made me think the bird I had seen was a female merlin.

I saw another strange bird in July.

July 5, 1976

This was my lucky night! I had been watching the snag for some time when a bird flew in, entered the cavity, then made its exit. I was confused. As the bird flew away it seemed smaller than the one I had seen in May, and rather than wearing a golden coat, it appeared darker in color with a prominently banded tail. Although the light was subdued I felt certain that this was not my golden bird. Later I found that the male merlin is smaller than the female. His back is slate gray in color and his tail is banded. The male merlin was doing the feeding tonight.

July 9, 1976

Today I watched what I interpreted as a threat display between the female merlin and a flicker. I had been waiting at the pond for some time when the merlin pair flew in and landed in the top of a big larch tree. Both birds sat preening in the sunlight. When a pair of flickers arrived a short time later one of the birds landed on the branch near the female merlin. The birds turned to face one another. Slowly, then, each bird extended its neck, elevated its tail and moved partially extended wings up and down. The actions of one bird seemed to mirror those of the other. In a matter of minutes the display ended and the flickers flew from the tree.

Since it seemed that the merlins planned to remain on their perches in the sunlight, I decided to walk closer. Neither bird appeared to notice my approach, nor did either bird watch me when I stood almost directly below them, staring up at their heads and streaked breasts. But when I walked slowly under them, then turned to look up at their tails, I found that both birds had turned on their branch. I was again looking up at heads and breasts. Neither bird flew to the snag during the time that I watched.

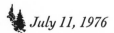 *July 11, 1976*

At seven the female merlin was in the cavity and seemed to be making no plans to leave. I walked over again about eleven. While I saw no feeding, I was able to watch the young birds as they moved about the cavity. One youngster walked to the doorway where it stood looking out over the water. Early in the afternoon I checked again; I saw no adults. About four I found a spot which was shaded from the hot sun and sat down to wait. The female merlin flew in, clung to the doorway braced by her long, banded tail, and looked into the cavity. Her color as I saw her today was a beautiful shade of rufous brown. She stayed on the snag only long enough to check the cavity, then flew away.

I was able to study both young merlins in the evening. They appeared to be slightly larger than an English sparrow. Their underparts were buff in color; the birds looked almost yellow in the evening light. Their heads were brown, or dark gray. The male merlin flew in silently, clung to the doorway and passed food to the young birds. In the failing light his back was moderately dark, his tail a lighter gray, banded with black.

July 12, 1976

Both young merlins stood in the doorway for a full hour this morning. During this time an adult merlin landed in a tall larch tree across the water, stayed there but a few minutes, then flew off. Some time later the female merlin arrived, looked into the cavity as she fluttered past, then landed in a tree nearby. She fluttered past the cavity two more times, then flew from the area. Fifteen minutes later she brought food, clung to the doorway but didn't enter the cavity. I watched the cavity for almost an hour tonight. During this time the female brought food one time. I didn't see the male.

July 15, 1976

I am told that even when one knows that a merlin is nesting somewhere in the area, it may be difficult to locate the nest. So I've been lucky! Although I made four trips to the snag today I saw no feedings. I did see the female merlin on two visits, however. Once she landed on the spire of a tall fir across the pond, did a slow turning in place as she studied the ground below. The second time I saw her she landed on a tall snag, again turned slowly as she scanned the ground. On neither occasion did she drop to the ground, nor did she visit the cavity. The youngsters have grown so large that only one can stand in the doorway at a time.

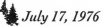 *July 17, 1976*

As I approached the pond at six this morning, eager to see activity at the home of the merlins, I heard a loud, piercing call I couldn't identify. The call was repeated over and over. When I located the bird, I found it to be one of the young merlins. I watched as it flew from tree to tree, finally landing in the top of a tall larch. The youngster flew well. It seemed less sure of its balance when the branch on which it landed bent under its weight, but quickly adjusted to the motion. This child appears to be smaller than the adult female, as I remember her. Its body, wings and tail seem more narrow than those of the adult. As the morning light improved I was able to see the buff-colored breast, and some of the markings about the head.

The young bird called continually for almost an hour. For much of this time it remained on the tall larch where I glassed it easily. Neither adult merlin appeared during this time. I could see nothing in the nest cavity as I passed, nor did I see the other young merlin.

July 18, 1976

Again this morning I heard the repeated calling of a young merlin. Again the bird landed on a branch in the crown of a larch. A robin carrying a worm in its bill flew from an adjacent tree, brushed the merlin from its perch, then flew on about its business elsewhere. The merlin flew to the top of another larch where it resumed its calling. I decided to wait, hoping that the cries of the young bird would bring an adult to the area. So that I might study the bird in greater comfort I moved to a spot of shade. There I suddenly realized I was looking at the second youngster. It sat, almost at eye level, on a stub projecting from the trunk of a lodgepole pine.

The bird was about twenty feet from me. It seemed dull when compared to its golden-colored sibling in the sunlight. Perched so close to the trunk of the tree with its wings pressed to its body, this youngster appeared to be smaller than the bird in the tree top. The back of this bird was dark brown, thinly streaked with black. Its exposed wing was dark gray. The face and neck were marked like those of the adult and the bill was the same shape, though smaller. The crown of its head was rufous. The buff-colored breast was heavily streaked. Its legs and the feet which gripped the perch were yellow.

This youngster showed no fear. It was most patient as I walked closer and moved about so that I might see it from several angles. As I moved the young bird followed me with its eyes. When it finally flew from its perch, the wing beats were regular and powerful. In flight it appeared to be twice the size of the bird I had seen on the perch. It made no sound in flight, and it flew low.

I hadn't excited this youngster, but it sure as hell had excited me! I couldn't believe my luck. My only regret was that it didn't join its sibling on the high larch in the sunlight. Some folks, it seems, are never satisfied.

Chapter Nine

FEEDERS

When I saw my first hummingbird it was displaying in a dive high over my tent. At that time I did not know what the bird was doing, what kind of hummer it was, or whether it was male or female. It was enough for me to know that I would see more of them. See more of them I did. Over a period of several years the hummingbirds increased in numbers from that single displaying male to swarms.

Initially the fighting that frequently takes place about my hummingbird feeders was worrisome to me, but I soon realized that in these battles few birds were injured unless they hit a window during the chase. Nor did any of the birds seem to go hungry because of the fighting. There were long periods here when these feisty little devils fed quietly, side by side.

Because the male hummingbird has no singing voice he must attract attention to himself in other ways. He does this by his sonorous flight and spectacular aerial display. Sounds accompanying these visual displays are said to be made by air passing through temporarily modified wing or tail feathers. I recall with pleasure the day I realized that I could tell whether a rufous or calliope hummingbird was diving by the sound made in the dive. The rufous male has still another way of winning female attention. Facing a female who has been cornered in the brush, he rapidly moves from side to side, covering a greater distance with his tail than he does with his head (a "whisk broom" display). The movement is so rapid that without the aid of slow motion photography it is difficult to be certain exactly what his movements are. This display amuses me but intimidates the female. As with life elsewhere, however, there always seems to be a female in the group who isn't taken in by male shenanigans.

In June of 1976, a female hummer seemed unimpressed by this rapid-fire display. The male displayed before a properly cornered female, but this girl was neither bewitched nor cowed. Suddenly she charged, forcing him back. Then she flew off with the male in pursuit. Like the "gone to fat" spectator at the ringside, I cheered!

At times this flashy show-off seems to waste a male bird's charm when there is no female about. I don't know whether at these times our boy is confused, or whether he can't control his good spirits. A few examples:

—A rufous male sat quietly on a branch in the feeder tree. Suddenly he noticed a junco feeding on a suet-seed block nearby. The hummer charged the feeder, drove the junco out the other side, and chased it three times around the feeder tree before the junco called it quits and settled on a branch. The cocky little rufous then displayed before the junco, flying the same rapid-fire display he uses to bewitch his females.

—I saw the rufous male displaying before a chipmunk.

—A mountain chickadee left her house and flew to a small fir tree. There she was seen by a rufous male who zoomed in and harassed her with his side-to-side display. When the chickadee moved to another tree, rufous moved with her. After five position changes, with five similar displays, I lost both the chickadee and her tormentor.

—Today I saw a rufous male practicing his rapid-fire display before a clump of grass. These beautiful little devils!

During some years the swarming of hummingbirds about the feeders was an impressive sight.

June 9, 1971

Late this evening I filled the hummer feeders. I stood under the tree for a time, looking, listening, disbelieving. There were birds everywhere! I felt as if a swarm of beautifully colored bees were playing about my head. There were birds at all feeders, birds diving, birds zooming and chasing. The feeder fir was loaded with "clicking" hummingbirds, and resting birds sat in the brush. When the last feeder was filled I stood holding it out at arm's length. Birds drank from it as long as I was able to hold it there, three or four birds drinking from the single-spouted feeder at the same time.

May 27, 1974

The activity about the hummingbird feeders must be seen to be believed. Last night I thought the birds were so active because I had too few feeders available. Tonight, with ten feeders hanging on the tree, the picture is the same. There are hummers feeding, sometimes six at a single spouted feeder, hummers zooming and chasing, birds resting on wires, in trees and brush, birds everywhere. Strangely there is little fighting.

May 29, 1975

The rufous male that commandeered the large feeder last night wasn't at his post tonight. There were so many feeders available for the swarming birds that only rarely did a hummer try to take syrup from the feeder he guarded. I suppose this wasn't an adequate challenge for him. Either he has joined the mob, or he has gone elsewhere. Tonight the hummers swarmed again. There were birds at all feeders, as many as six drinking from a single spouted feeder. There were eighteen of these feeders hanging on the feeder fir, plus one large feeder. As I stood beneath the tree I thought I heard my first Swainson's thrush of the season, but the sound of hummer wings in motion about me and the clicking sounds made by the resting birds interfered with my reception of other sounds.

The feeder fir is far enough from the cabin that only rarely does a bird in flight hit a window.

May 16, 1973

I stood near the feeding area during a pitched battle tonight. A bird hit the window, then landed at my feet. The calliope male was being chased by a rufous male who landed on the walk, glared at the injured bird, then zoomed away. The stunned calliope stood braced on either side by a wing. His chin rested on the toe of my boot. He was groggy and confused, but very much alive. He recovered slowly, looked up at me, finally zoomed away. What a headache that bird must have!

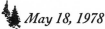 *May 18, 1978*

I heard a soft thud made by a small bird as it hit the window, went out and picked up a rufous male. The only sign of life as I held the bird in the palm of my hand was the infrequent blinking of his eyelids. He lay quietly, legs held tightly against his body, toes clamped together making feet like little black balls. The orange-red feathers at his throat glowed in the subdued light. His back, a beautiful shade of brownish red, showed only one small area of green. I sat for a long time holding the bird, enjoying his beauty, but seeing few signs of life. Suddenly a spell of rapid, shallow breathing caused a quivering of the brilliant feathers at his throat. Another period of quiet followed, during which the only movement I could see was the extension and retraction of his long, needle-like tongue. Finally his eyelids opened widely and he seemed to be watching the movement of my hand as I stroked his feathers with my finger. His feet opened; his toes clutched my finger. Then his eyelids blinked at regular intervals. After a long period of inactivity the little beauty shot from my hand and zoomed away. He flew low, but well.

One day in the middle of August four birds hovered in position before a single spouted feeder. A bird left the line, flew to the feeder, and drank. When it had finished drinking the hummer flew backward to its original position. The next bird flew in, drank and returned to position, again flying backward. When the third and fourth birds had had their innings, the first bird flew to drink again. This little game, and game it must have been, continued for several minutes.

A short time later two birds that had been dive-bombing one another at the feeders hovered in the air facing one another. Then maintaining these positions they rose as if in an elevator, stopping at each floor before they continued upward. They were still facing each other with bills almost touching when they were well up in the sky.

Four years later on a hot day in June I saw two hummingbirds playing a similar game. There had been no activity about the feeders during the day, but when the evening began to cool the hummers came in to feed. Again I saw two birds hovering in place as they faced each other with bills almost touching. Again the birds rose as if in an elevator, but at each stop tonight they rotated, still in position, as if on a lazy-Susan. After two or three revolutions they resumed their ascent. This game continued through six stops, then the formation dissolved and the birds flew down to feed.

Occasionally a hummingbird, usually a male but either rufous or calliope, will take on human quarry in its play. I find, too, that at times the birds are very curious. A few examples:

—A male calliope charged me two times, both times as if he were planning on passing straight through me. He circled my head and with each succeeding circle he flew closer to me. I didn't move. He flew to my glasses, hovering there as he looked into both of my eyes before zooming away.

—I stood near the cabin watching the birds at the feeders. A hummingbird flew in from behind. It hovered about my head as it examined my hair, my neck, both ears and my cheeks. The temptation to turn my head to look at the bird was almost overpowering. I knew, though, that if I turned, the bird would zoom away. The sound made by the hovering bird as it flew about my ears was incredibly loud. Its curiosity satisfied, the hummer flew to the cabin where it examined the window and the log walls. It was a male calliope.

—A rufous male flew to me as I stood watching the birds at the feeders. I didn't move as he inserted his bill into each nostril, then into each ear canal. His curiosity satisfied, he shot back to the feeders.

At noon one day, when I filled the feeders the hummers completely ignored me, zooming about my head as if I were not there. When I reached up to hang the two feeders I had just filled, the birds started feeding before I had hung either of them. I had a delightful view of the rufous male as he fed from the hand-held feeder, at the beauty of his rufous-colored body feathers, and the jewel-like feathers at his throat. He fed alone at his feeder and was very thirsty. He stayed there drinking for some time.

Have you ever tried your hand at the study of avian behavior? Such attempts on my part have been both amusing, confusing, and rarely enlightening. I began my study with ravens. Early one October while riding through the forest, I came upon a flock of ravens as they sat in conference on a logging road. A large delegation from the flock followed us home. Since my companions Piccolo, the mare, and Penny, the elkhound, were young and very much alive, this peculiar behavior on the part of the large, black birds indicated that it must be the master who looked like carrion. Who am I to question the inborn judgment of ravens? I wondered if this resemblance to carrion was a recent change, or if old friends had been unusually kind?

One stormy afternoon late in the hunting season a number of these birds followed again, screaming invectives as they circled Penny and me as we hiked down a logging road. I began to wonder, then, if the ravens had been conditioned to expect every human to scatter entrails about the countryside. Perhaps they were surprised to see a two-legged being so far from a motor vehicle.

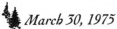 *March 30, 1975*

When a raven pair flew in this morning one of the big birds picked an ancient dog bone from a pile of snow left by the plow, then hopped with it to the rail fence. There it sat on the top rail, picking at the bone as if there were still bits of meat left on its surface. The second raven flew to the fence, sat beside its friend, and attempted to share in the find. But the bird with the bone would have none of that; it dropped to the ground with its treasure. A moment later the second raven dropped to the ground where it stood for a time studying the back of the greedy bird. Then, having decided on a course of action, it moved stealthily toward the rear of the busily pecking raven. With one quick movement it reached under the tail and between the legs of the preoccupied bird, snatched the bone, and flew away with it. The astonished dispossessed raven watched the retreating bird until it disappeared from view. Then, with a shrug, it, too, flew from the meadow.

These big, black, intelligent, noisy clowns can be extremely graceful in flight. I think of the hot day late in July when I decided to loll on Cedar Peak in the northern Missions, rather than dropping to the unnamed lakes below as I had planned. Horseflies were numerous enough to be annoying, but not annoying enough to drive me from the peak. I was looking toward the more rugged mountains in the southern Missions when a flock of ten ravens rose on an updraft behind me and treated me to an aerial ballet. Watching as the birds rose on updrafts or soared above me without apparent effort or movement of wings was the day's highlight. They seemed to be having so much fun. Occasionally one of the big birds dropped toward the peak as if it were planning to land, then, when the dogs came running, moved out in an easy, soaring glide. Only the dogs didn't realize that they were being baited. The flock soared about us for some time, dropping out of sight behind the mountain now and then, always riding the updraft on their return.

Other birds entertain. I sometimes meet the Clark's nutcracker when I wander in the high country in summer. Members of the crow family, these birds with their predominantly light gray bodies, black wings, and black tail frequently appear at the valley feeders in winter. They are gluttons when suet is available; where they feed, they rule. In my experience the nutcracker is a highly intelligent bird. As evidence I submit the following notes from my journal.

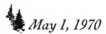 *May 1, 1970*

These resourceful nutcrackers! Much of their winter is spent carrying suet from the metal basket to storage places known only to themselves. Today, when the supply of suet ran low in the basket, one of the birds decided to rob a tiny cup of once melted suet which I had hung near the tip of a branch in the feeder fir for use of the smaller birds. I watched as the nutcracker slowly moved sideways toward the end of an adjacent, but higher, branch. As the bird moved outward the branch on which it stood bent under its weight, bringing it down almost to the level of the feeder cup. Now the bird leaned backward as it continued to move outward. This brought the branch on which it was standing both downward and forward. When branch and cup touched, the bird quickly flexed its toes, clasping the rim of the cup to the branch on which it was standing. Both branches were now immobilized, and the nutcracker was ready for business.

After the greedy bird had eaten its fill and flown away, I checked the branch on which it had been standing. To make the maneuver possible the bird had nipped two small shoots from the branch on which it had walked. The big bird repeated the maneuver several times during the rest of the day. Wondering just how this intelligent bird might meet another challenge, I removed the small branch it had used in its approach to the suet cup. I saw the bird feeding from another small branch. Here, however, it fed with difficulty as it was unable to stabilize branch and cup. When its thrust was too vigorous the bird lost its balance. But tonight the nutcracker was back in business. Carefully it worked its way along a different branch. Again it leaned backward so that its weight drove the branch toward the suet cup. When the branch was close to the feeder, the nutcracker grasped the rim of the cup with its bill, pulled the cup toward its foot, then held cup and branch in contact with its toes. Eating again presents few problems. There shall be no further interference; this bird deserves its reward.

Two other members of the crow family seem unlikely play-
mates, yet they frequently visit the feeding area together. The
dark, brassy Steller's jay with its raucous calls always rules
the feeding area when the nutcrackers are not there. The
gray jay, equally greedy but more likable, waits its turn at
the feeder, a turn which may be slow in arriving if there are
many Steller's jays in the group. The inroads that these large
birds made in the available food supplies were formidable,
especially when I was still trying to feed doughnuts to the
smaller birds. For this reason I spent much time designing
feeders that I hoped the larger birds would be unable to use.

Steller's jays, by their numbers alone, frequently kept gray
jays from the feeder. Yet both types of birds flew in to feed at
the same time. When there were fewer Steller's jays about,
the rules of the eating game changed. A gray jay, watched by
two or three Steller's, was allowed to take bread from the
feeder, but as it flew away with its loot it was followed by the
scolding, dark blue bandits. The nervous gray jay invariably
dropped its bread square, which was then snatched from the
ground by one of the raucous birds. Only when the Steller's
jays tired of the play were the gray jays allowed to feed.

I recall with pleasure the day when this show took a new
turn. A gray jay had taken bread but, as usual, had dropped
it in flight. One of the scolding bullies swooped to the ground,
picked up the bread, and flew off. This left two alert Steller's
jays waiting near the feeder. The gray jay flew back to the
feeder. Stood on its rim for a moment, then deliberately
dropped one square of bread over the side. One of the waiting bandits dropped to the ground, snatched the food, and
flew away. After a moment's wait a second piece fell to the

ground. The second Steller's jay flew away with this prize. Then the victimized bird leisurely chose two squares for itself and flew from the feeding area. Good planning, gray jay!

The adult jays quickly learned that they could not use the smaller birds' doughnut feeder because of the narrow spaces between the wires in the cage—but then along came their babies.

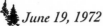 *June 19, 1972*

In the past the spaces in the protective cage that hangs over the doughnut feeder have been too narrow to permit passage of larger birds. But this summer I widened four spaces so that the western tanager might use the feeder. When the gray jays proudly brought their recently fledged youngsters to the feeding area today the adults ignored the doughnut feeder. However, the young birds (who were equally as large as their parents) had not learned that this food was inaccessible to them. Both young birds quickly found the widened spaces and are now happily feeding on doughnuts.

The atmosphere of the feeding area may change from one of peace and serenity to one of violence in a matter of seconds. For a few weeks each summer the western tanager lends its color and song to my peace and happiness. I watch with pleasure as that spot of color flies toward the feeding area. I listen to its song before and after feeding, then see the bird fly back to its home and family. For some reason the colorful male tanager feeds on syrup more frequently than its mate, but both male and female come regularly for doughnuts. This pleasant scene changed when unpaired tanagers met at the feeder; there was likely to be trouble.

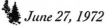

June 27, 1972

The tanagers demanded their share of attention today. This morning two males met at the syrup where they fought at the feeders then chased each other through the timber. Finally both birds flew away without either eating or drinking. This afternoon I saw them again. Another battle started with one male inside the doughnut feeder, the other outside. They fought for several minutes, then, to my surprise, suddenly changed places; one bird left the cage as the other entered. The battle was resumed as if there had been no interruption.

June 2, 1973

Tonight I sat near the cabin prepared to enjoy the birds at the feeders. Things went smoothly for a time, then four pairs of tanagers arrived for doughnuts at the same time. There was fighting between males, fighting between females, and fighting between male and female. Birds inside the cage fought with birds outside the cage. At one time a female tanager calmly ate doughnut while two males fought in the cage beside her. The fighting became so disturbing to me that when the doughnut feeder was empty I didn't refill it. I reasoned that if there was no food to fight over each pair would go its separate way. Not so! The females did fly from the feeding area, but the males stayed. They fought over the empty feeder, they battled over the syrup dish, and one male tanager attempted to drive the hummingbirds from their feeders.

One day early in June as I was working on the woodpile I heard a tanager sing as it flew in to feed. Its song finished, the colorful male dropped to the syrup cup which at that moment was completely framed by white serviceberry blossoms. There the bird sang again before it drank, its song of thanks offered as it flew from the feeder. An exquisite setting for a colorful bird.

Feeding birds played a skit before an audience of one on a morning in July. I had become accustomed to seeing adult sapsuckers feeding from the syrup cup, but on that morning a young sapsucker, large as an adult, flew in alone. For a time it went from tree to tree, staring at the feeder each time it landed on a trunk. The youngster seemed afraid to fly to the freely-swinging feeder. Finally it flew, but an adult had arrived and was now drinking syrup. The young bird made a successful landing, but in doing so knocked its parent from the feeder. It stood upright for a brief moment, clutching the rim of the glass cup in desperation, then lost its balance and started falling backward. When its body came to rest the bird hung upside down, still clutching the rim of the feeder. It hung like this for some time, then with a great heave, it brought its body up to a standing position. The young bird stayed on the feeder for a long time, obviously intending to collect its reward.

One summer I discovered both a heron colony and an active osprey nest on the west side of the Swan River. The great blue herons had built their nests on the branches of a tall, but topless, ponderosa pine; the osprey nested on the top of a tall snag nearby. I could watch all nests from the same overlook. In many hours spent watching these birds, I had never seen a feeding in the heron colony.

August 20, 1976

I had spent an unexciting hour glassing the heron colony and the osprey nest. Then, while walking back to the vehicle, I heard an uproar that just had to be the table-talk of a family of herons. As I charged back to the over-look the din became louder, and when I broke into the open I found the north nest in a state of confusion. All I could see there was a mass of bodies and wildly flapping wings. I worried that one of the young birds might be pushed over the side of the nest. The action was too fast and the distance between us too great for me to see de-tails of this feeding, but what I did see provided a great thrill. Suddenly the adult struggled free of the mass and quickly flew from the nest. Young birds in other nests in the colony were in a state of excitement; not until the re-cently fed young birds relaxed did the colony return to normal.

Feedings in osprey nests are much more casual. I watched one day as a female osprey sat brooding her eggs, looking out at the world below. When the male flew in he dropped a fish in front of his mate, then hopped to his usual perch above the nest. No audible thank you was offered; none seemed to be expected. The female tore her fish apart and ate quietly. Even after there are young in the nest of the osprey the ar-rival of the male with lunch causes little excitement. With no wasted effort both female and young eat their meal.

I have usually seen these big birds going separate ways without appearing to notice one another. Only once have I seen amusing by-play between them. On my arrival that day, there seemed to be more coming and going of the big birds than usual, although it was still a restful scene. Suddenly, and with no warning, an osprey dove at a heron perched on a tall snag. I'm not certain whose surprise was the greater, the heron's or my own. The act, which was not repeated, appeared to have been done in fun.

The great blue heron is a study in patience when fishing.

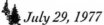 *July 29, 1977*

Early this morning I stood on the shore of a large pond checking ducks on the water. A great blue heron flew in and landed on a partially submerged log at the opposite end of the pond. There it posed for what seemed like a very long time. Finally the big bird stepped off the log and with almost imperceptible movement worked its way along the shore in the water. The heron had stopped moving and was slowly lowering its head toward the water when a noisy kingfisher landed on a branch nearby. The big bird looked up, apparently annoyed. Then, as if trying to make its intrusion felt more keenly, the kingfisher dove into the water near the heron.

Quiet was just returning to that end of the pond when the resident goldeneye hen made an attack on a large young duck of another family. This attack, one in which there was real body contact, riled the water near the heron for a second time. The big bird stood quietly for several minutes, then again started inching its way along the shore. I could be certain that the heron had stopped moving only when its head moved slowly toward the water. Suddenly the bird struck. Ponderously, then, it took off from the water and flew out over the trees.

For me the sound of the loon is the living symbol of the wild, enchanting, north country. I recall the moonlit night when I first heard the tremolo of a loon call. I was camped on a rocky island in the Boundary Waters Canoe Area of Minnesota. The moon was full; the birds were not far off shore. I sat for a long, long time, leaning against a tree trunk, looking out over the quiet water. Not a sound could be heard other than the singing of the loon. Occasionally a bird drifted effortlessly across the silver streak of moonlight. Finally I caught myself dozing, the fatigue of a pleasurable day's paddling asserting itself. I crawled into the sleeping bag and fell asleep to the song of the loon.

In Montana, on a morning in June I dropped by trail to a large subalpine lake in the Missions. I sat on a boulder at the edge of the water, listening to the soft splashing of waves against rock, looking toward the slabs and the peaks of the Mission divide at the end of the lake, relaxing and dreaming before lunch. My two friends lay on the shore, dog-dreaming. The call of a loon on the water nearby surprised me; I hadn't seen the bird's approach. Each time this loon gave its wild, beautiful call it dunked its head in the water as the call was ending; each lovely call ended in a gurgle. When the bird lifted its head out of the water its next call had already started. I was fascinated; I had never before seen this display.

After a long period of calling I saw two loons swimming toward us from the distant end of the lake. Soon I had three loons calling on the water near me. All three birds ended each call with their heads below the surface of the lake. Finally this period of harmonizing was over and there was chasing on the water. The change was so sudden and the action so fast that I couldn't be certain whether one bird was being threatened, or whether all three were enjoying the action.

There was another period of calling after which, to my regret, all three birds swam against the waves toward the mountains at the end of the lake. The wild, melodious calling of loons in surroundings of such beauty had been mesmerizing. Not even the searing heat during our climb back up the mountain detracted from the pleasures of the day.

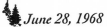 *June 28, 1968*

It was about mid-afternoon on western Montana's first annual "loon day." We were hot and weary as we clambered down a short, steep bank toward our last assigned lake of the day. A pair of loons on the water heard us coming; they started calling even before we walked out of the timber. The loons continued their wild serenade as they swam toward us. Gradually they stopped moving but continued calling for some time. Across the lake, going its own silent way, was their one, half-grown chick. Forming a backdrop for this family group was the lovely Swan Range. With eyes glued to the binoculars, spiritually renewed, and somehow even less hot and weary, we sat quietly for a time. Gradually the birds became silent, but they didn't leave us. They resumed their calling as we walked back into the timber on our way to the vehicle.

The other birds in this high valley are rarely so haunting. During my first winter on this property, mountain chickadees held a sliding party in the bird-feeding area near my cabin. After a heavy snowfall that left roofs, fences, trees, and brush snow-covered and mountain peaks under a heavy white blanket, a dozen chickadees exchanged winter worries for a moment of play. Each bird started on the topmost branch of a snow-loaded fir. The bird slid down the branch, gaining momentum by flapping its wings, much as it would if it were bathing in a puddle or taking a dust bath. When a bird reached the tip of the slippery branch, it dropped to the branch below and continued its slide. When the birds reached the lowest branch on the tree they flew back to the feeder for a snack.

During lunch another winter day I heard the soft thud of a small bird hitting the window. I found the injured chickadee sitting quietly on the rim of the wrought-iron suet basket that hung on a tree near the cabin. The chick faced me with eyes closed. Obviously stunned by the blow, it remained in this position for several minutes during which time I stood at the window and worried. As I watched, a second chickadee flew in and dropped to the side of the injured bird. The new arrival stared at its friend for some time, then threw back its head and called loudly, four times. The fourth call brought a response from the dazed chickadee. Its eyes opened; it moved its head slowly from side to side. The two birds flew off together.

EPILOGUE

I fell in love with Montana's mountains the first time I saw them. I knew then that some day I would live here. My vacation time was frequently spent touring the West until I learned that neophytes like me could, for a price, join guided trips into wilderness areas. On these pack trips dudes rode horses, their duffel was carried by pack string, and the food was good. Usually when on these outings I worked and rode with the crew; I learned more that way. Finally, I bought an old homestead at Condon in the Swan Valley, deciding to exchange my job as an M.D. in a Midwestern clinic for a more physically demanding one in the out-of-doors.

We've seen many changes in the valley since 1965. Should you visit, the overcutting of forests and resulting clearcuts will probably be the first of these changes to catch your eye. Clearcuts that have been planted now resemble tree farms, but they do provide cover for wildlife and in the distant future may be ready for harvest. They are known as "plantations." Regeneration in some of the unplanted clearcuts has been slow. One also sees more homes in the valley now, some of which are in small subdivisions. We also have a new post office, two improved markets, a church or two, eating establishments, and four bars.

None of the residents of Condon can prove exactly where our town is. A few years ago the Montana Department of Highways decided to locate Condon for the convenience of tourists. The crew chose what they thought were proper places for two highway signs, dug the holes, sunk the posts, attached the signs, and drove off, another job done. A night or two later a local sorehead who didn't agree with the location of either sign cranked up his chain saw and sawed them both down. Rumor has it that the Department of Highways admits defeat; they have vowed that they will never try to locate the village of Condon again.